Thomas Gage in Spanish America

Thomas Gage receiving gifts from his parishioners—a completely fanciful picture
from the first German edition of the *English-American*

THOMAS GAGE
IN SPANISH AMERICA

by

Norman Newton

FABER AND FABER
24 Russell Square
London

First published in 1969
by Faber and Faber Limited
24 Russell Square London WC1
Printed in Great Britain by
Butler & Tanner Ltd Frome and London
All rights reserved

S.B.N. 571 08799 X

Contents

Illustrations

New Spain in the seventeenth century

Preface

THOMAS GAGE was in many ways an unpleasant person. But he was, in most things, a candid one, and it is this relative honesty—not only about himself as a person, but also about the things he saw and heard—which makes him such a good travel writer.

Gage, who came of a distinguished family of English Roman Catholics, was a Dominican friar in 1625, when he volunteered to go to the Philippines as a missionary. In Mexico, however, he decided to run away from the Philippine mission. For twelve years he served as a priest in Guatemala, returning to England in 1637. In England, he left his church, flirted briefly with Anglicanism, and joined the Parliamentarians. His conversion to radical Protestantism, and the influences of a time of moral confusion, seem to have caused what must be called a moral breakdown. His testimony in court was responsible for putting a brother in prison, and sending three priests to their deaths.

In 1648, Gage published a book on his travels, which led to his becoming involved in Cromwell's invasion of Hispaniola and Jamaica in 1655. He died in Jamaica early in 1656.

Gage's book—*The English–American His Travel by Sea and Land, or A New Survey of the West Indies*—appeared at a time when Spanish Mexico, or New Spain, was hardly better known to Englishmen than the Aztec Empire had been. At this time, the long-festering desire of English merchants and statesmen to seize the Spanish colonies in America, or, failing

9

that, to gain control of their economies, was reaching a climax. That 'mechanic fellow', Cromwell (the phrase is Charles the Second's), was in this, though he was so virulent an enemy of many more benign traditions, continuing the foreign policy of Elizabeth the First. Perhaps it would be more correct to say that he was continuing the foreign policy of the Elizabethan merchant class. It was during this time— the Cromwellian interregnum—that the English, who had up to then been forced to content themselves with piracy, laid the foundation of their Caribbean Empire. Gage's book afforded some of the arguments in justification of this venture. In 1655—the year in which Gage himself participated in Cromwell's invasion of Hispaniola and Jamaica—the book was reprinted. And in 1677, Colbert, who had his own 'Western Design', ordered a French translation prepared.

It is not difficult to see why the book should have been so popular in countries which had aggressive designs against the Spanish Empire. It had great propaganda value. It showed that the Spaniards were oppressing the Indians, and that any attempt to 'liberate' them, that is, oppress them oneself, could be justified in the highest moral terms. It was easy enough for the Puritans to forget that their own record in America was, in most respects, much less distinguished. Furthermore, the book was an admirable piece of reconnaissance. Gage seems to have gone out of his way to observe and describe just those things which an invading army would have had to be aware of—roads, harbours, and fortifications. He also noted those sensitive areas of political and religious life which might be expected to harbour possibilities of subversion.

Gage was not a very good writer: his evangelical moralizings sit oddly in a literary style which tends towards a dusty Baroque floridity. But he had marvellous eyes and ears, and a keen sense of social structure, and there is a vivid plain accuracy beneath the somewhat repellent surface of his style. His cool and accurate picture of the country, vivid in detail and precise in its statement of the more general aspects of the culture, reminds one of the water-colours and plans of eighteenth-century army officers.

There seems to be general agreement that, in his descriptions of physical things at least, Gage is to be trusted. Indeed, in most studies of seventeenth-century New Spain, Gage is quoted as an authority, along with Spanish governmental and ecclesiastical documents of the time.

There are certain omissions, of course. Gage makes little mention of the arts of seventeenth-century Mexico, except as examples of the extravagance and wantonness of the society. It should be pointed out, therefore, that this was—considering the size of the population involved—perhaps the most artistically productive period in the history of post-Columbian America. Poets such as Bernardo de Balbuena, Francisco de Terrazas, Fray Miguel de Guevara, Luis de Sandoval y Zapata, and, above all, Sor Juana Ines de la Cruz; playwrights such as Juan Ruiz de Alarcón, arguably the greatest dramatist ever to come out of America; the historians of the Conquest and the pre-Columbian civilizations; the composers Franco, Fructos del Castillo, Bermudez and Padilla; the architects and craftsmen who built the great cathedrals and buildings of state: these created in Mexico a Renaissance and Baroque culture of distinction and nobility. It was, of course, provincial to that of Spain, but its splendour was no less great for that. Furthermore, it was a distinctly American Renaissance and Baroque, in which elements from Europe and pre-Columbian America were joined to form a new whole.

Gage tells a number of stories about events in which he

was not personally involved: these are vivid little pictures of Mexican life, and, far from being digressions, they are essential to his picture of New Spain. He was, among other things, a born gossip.

What are we to make of Gage's accounts of the state of religion in America? J. E. S. Thompson, the distinguished United States archaeologist, holds, in his edition of *The English–American* (entitled *Thomas Gage's Travels in the New World*), that they are highly exaggerated and unfair; Gage's other editor, A. P. Newton, seems to accept them as fair accounts of the situation. Certainly, there was much to admire in the Roman Catholicism of Baroque Spanish America, and Gage—anti-Papist as only a convert to Protestantism can be—has nothing to say in favour of Rome. Yet he is careful, by and large, to stick to the facts: all the abuses he recounts can be found in the records of Mexican civil and ecclesiastical courts. To readers nurtured on tales of Spanish cruelties, his account must have seemed rather mild: they would have expected stories of genocide and atrocity, and instead he told tales of venality, greed and deceit—lesser, rather unexciting crimes.

The fact is that, in its stated intentions at least, the Spanish Church showed itself to be as enlightened as any of the other churches of seventeenth-century Christendom. Even the Inquisition, cruel as it was, was not more cruel than the anti-Papist tribunals of Protestant Europe. Nor is the record of the Spanish government dishonourable. A degree of respect was shown towards those native institutions not inextricably bound up with the horrible Aztec religion, and it was held as a point of doctrine that the Indians were, as much as the Spaniards, rational men. But these doctrines were quietly set to one side by the conquistadores, settlers and merchants, who, like other colonial élites in North and

South America, had the rapacity and greed of the new rich. They had, very quickly, won the power and prestige of landed aristocrats, without having inherited that tradition of moral responsibility which had softened the European feudal system. In these qualities, many of the Mexican clergy and friars seem to have differed from the rich land-owners not in kind, but only in degree—in their rejection of the more odious forms of physical coercion, and in the fact that they tended to extort and oppress as corporate bodies rather than as individuals.

Yet the evils of the society—real enough—should not be exaggerated. The Mexican countryside was bountiful in a way which we, used to a rural life denatured and impoverished by the tumour-like growth of the manufacturing industries, can hardly imagine. (The average Indian peasant was certainly better off than the English factory worker of the early 1800's.) The Anglo-Saxon reader, his imagination fed at several removes by reworkings of Las Casas' account of the horrors committed by the Spaniards in the West Indies, tends to think of the Spanish Empire as infamously cruel. In fact, Las Casas exaggerated without scruple: one Spanish scholar, Ramon Menéndez Pidal, has argued convincingly that he was a paranoid, though a well-intentioned one. The first settlement of the West Indies, by a population many of whom were not Christians, and in which criminals, vagabonds and profiteers were more than adequately represented, was certainly accompanied by horrors of every kind; but then so was the settling by Anglo-Saxons of Newfoundland, Australia and California. After this dark period, the Spanish Empire was, in Mexico at least, no more cruel towards the indigenous inhabitants than most empires have been. Indeed, except for certain Creoles 'in advance of their time', the Spaniards were not racially prejudiced in the

modern sense. The mixture of the conquering and indigenous races was the announced aim of Spanish and Papal
policy in the late 1500's. Theirs was a caste, not a racist
society. Gage, who is hardly a friendly observer, finds much
brutal exploitation of Indians and negroes, but he gives only
a few examples of wanton sadism, all of them, as even he
points out, in clear violation of Spanish law.

It is interesting to discover in Gage evidence of the bitter
hostility felt by the Creoles towards the mother country, a
feeling which had become apparent even before the Conquest was completed. A similar feeling was found in the
colonies of Britain and France—one need only mention the
Barbados revolt of 1652, the unrest in Jamaica during the
1720's, the conflict between the merchant seigneurs of New
France and the metropolitan government of France, and
the mercantile dissatisfactions which, fed by dreams of a
New World Order, brought about the revolt of the Thirteen
Colonies. In Mexico, as in the rest of America, a colonial
slave-owning and trading class was restive under the re-
straints—many of them just—imposed upon it by the
government of the home country. Yet curiously, and perhaps this is simply due to the relative prosperity of Mexico,
there were no open separatist revolts, such as there were, for
instance, in Catalonia.

There is one regrettable omission in Gage's book: he never
tells us what he looks like. Thus there moves through his
world of vivid sights, smells and sounds, long since dissipated,
a figure who must be for us, in visual terms, an ambulant
void.

I must say, to conclude this preface, that I have not felt
myself bound by Gage's terminology: for example, he refers,
not to 'Mexico City', but to 'Mexico', a usage which would
only be confusing, since the word now means, to most

English-speakers, the country rather than the city. I have called the capital 'Mexico City' for the sake of clarity, even though this is anachronistic.

Currency comparisons are based on figures given by Gage himself. I have not come across any comparative study of seventeenth-century Mexican and English currency values, or any detailed comparison of relative costs of living. It must be remembered here that a unit of money would have bought much more in his century than it will buy in ours.

I—*The Missionary*

In less than two months, the galleon fleet would be sailing for America. Friar Antonio Calvo was busy. He had to find six Dominicans in the monasteries of Andalucia, six friars willing to travel halfway round the world, to serve their order, and Christ, in the Philippines. They must be ready to leave Cadiz in the first week of July. In Cadiz, they would join twenty-four friars recruited in the cloisters of Castile and the vicinity of Madrid by the man under whose orders Calvo was acting—the Pope's Commissary for the Dominican Mission to the Philippines, Friar Mateo de la Villa.

Thus, around the end of May, 1625, his quota almost made up from the friaries of Cordova, Seville and San Lucar, Friar Antonio came to the Dominican convent at Jerez. With him he had one Father Antonio Meléndez, of the College of St Gregory in the northern Spanish town of Valladolid.

In that convent, Meléndez was greatly surprised and pleased to discover an acquaintance of his, a one-time fellow student in the College of St Gregory. This was the Englishman Thomas Gage—Friar Tomás de Santa Maria. Gage was then about twenty-three years of age; he was a restless young man, fonder of travel than of study, and less fond of the contemplative life than of either of these. Meléndez took it on himself to persuade the English friar to join the Philippine mission. Since he had been given a good supply of money to cover his travelling expenses, he decided to begin by buying Gage a good supper: the Englishman enjoyed food, and did not much relish friary fare. Not that this was mere policy on Meléndez' part; he was an open-hearted man; he wished to share some of his money with his friend, and his own enthusiasm for the Philippine adventure was quite genuine. The 'good Jerez sack', which, Gage tells us with retroactive disapproval, 'was not spared', inspired him to declaim, almost rhapsodically, about the glories of this country which he had not seen.

He began, decorously and conventionally enough, with the glories of possible martyrdom. One need only be killed by a pagan to achieve eternal glory. Should he, Meléndez, have the good fortune to die converting the Japanese, they would make a book of his life and death; and though he was only the son of a Segovia tailor, the Holy Father would call him St Anthony, and talk of him in the same breath as the Apostles in Heaven.

As the level of the sack crept down the bottle, his rhapsody became somewhat more secular in character, though its tone was occasionally elevated by a reference to Scripture. Had Gage heard, he asked, of the riches of the Philippines? Why, the sails of their ships were not made of coarse canvas, but of Chinese silk! Pearls, rubies and diamonds were there considered mere pretty stones. They paved the ground with tiles of gold and silver. One might consider the islands the true Promised Land: the trees were hung with clusters of nutmegs bigger than the bunches of grapes Joshua and Caleb had brought back from Canaan, and their chocolate, sweetened with sugar from the canes in their fields, tasted like milk and honey.

As the wine-bottle emptied, Meléndez' dream of the Philippines became more and more profane. The land was an Earthly Paradise, a Garden of Pleasures. There every Adam could have his Eve, with no fruit forbidden, for what was a

18

sin in Spain was there only the custom of the country. And wherever a lucky friar might travel, there would be 'Indians' to sound trumpets before him; they would strew flowers beneath the hooves of his horses; they would put up triumphal arches for him; and they would kneel before him as if he were a god.

Will you come with me, Thomas?—he said as they parted, and swore that he would not sleep that night until he knew they would be setting out together. He left Gage with six Spanish pistoles, and a promise that if he could steel himself to face the pleasant martyrdom he had described, Calvo would give him more than enough money to buy supplies for that long and tedious journey, which would take him across two oceans and the breadth of New Spain.

Gage's reply was cautious: he said he would sleep on it. But, he added, he would do much for his old friend. If he did decide to go, he would try to persuade a friend at that convent, the Irish friar, Tomás de León, to accompany him.

Even after one had made allowances for Meléndez' naïve enthusiasm, there was much in the Philippines to attract a young friar anxious to get ahead. Manila was then the centre of trade and missionary activity in Spain's Far Eastern Empire, and in Manila there were two classes of importance, the merchants and the friars. When they were engaged together in the profitable task of spreading civilization and Christianity, it was sometimes hard to tell them apart. Overseas trade was an obsession in that city, which Father Chirino described as 'a copy of that Tyre so praised by Ezekiel'. Agriculture was left to the native Filipinos, and local retail trade and the mechanical arts to the Chinese. Persons of importance in the city devoted themselves to buying goods from the Chinese and Japanese ships which visited Manila each year for the trade fair, and shipping them on, at an appropriate mark-up, to Acapulco. Through Manila came many of those Oriental goods which were becoming essential to the happiness and comfort of the wealthy classes of America and Europe. There were luxury goods, staples and trivia—Chinese silks, fine cottons from India, Persian rugs and carpets, porcelain vessels, spices, gold bullion, jewels, fans, eyeglasses, paper balloons, musk, slaves from South Africa, red lead, tea and copper spittoons.

The religious houses were the banks of the colony, and their interest rates were exorbitant. Practically, this was justified by the dangers of the Pacific crossing; the lingering moral doubts of an age which still retained something of the old fear that usury was a sin against nature were assuaged by the fact that the money the houses earned, in their capacity as commercial banks and marine insurance companies, went to charitable foundations, the *obras pias*, or 'pious works'. The religious orders were almost all-powerful. Rather later than the period in which this book is set, three of the governors of the Philippines were brutally humiliated by the orders: one was first removed from his position, then made to stand every day in the streets of Manila; one was broken by the Holy Inquisition; one was slaughtered by a mob incited by friars.

Gage lay awake most of that night, trying to make up his mind. In the Philippines, he would undoubtedly rise in the Church much more quickly than he would in Spain; he might, indeed, come to live the life of a potentate. On the other hand, he might die at sea, be eaten by cannibals, or die miserably of disease in some wretched cluster of grass huts, stinking of dung and decayed vegetation. In Spain, however, he would probably always remain a poor friar, unless, indeed, he were to be sent back to England as a clandestine priest, to live a hole-and-corner life which might

20

end at any time in the ambiguous triumph of a martrydom. Gage came from a line of martyrs, it is true; but he was the weak member of the family.

He had been away from home ten years or so, having left at the age of about thirteen years to go to the Jesuit college for English boys at St Omer, near Calais. He came from a distinguished and rather dangerous family of country squires, which had risen from obscurity in Tudor times.

He was related, though very remotely, to a number of distinguished persons in the aristocracy and minor gentry, among them Sir Francis Bacon (Lord Verulam), the Earl of Salisbury Sir Robert Cecil, Henry Wriothesley the Earl of Southampton, and also, though the connection was so remote as to be almost meaningless, with William Shakespeare. (In order to avoid misunderstandings, I should hasten to show just how remote this last connection was. The grand-aunt of Robert Southwell, his mother's cousin, was the daughter of Nicholas 1st Lord Vaux, whose other daughter, Catherine, had married Sir George Throckmorton, whose grand-daughter, Mary Throckmorton, had married Edward Arden, son of William Arden, who was third cousin to Shakespeare's mother.)

Gage's great-grandfather had served Henry VIII, when the Church of England had rejected the suzerainty of the Pope, but not the Catholic faith; he had been in disfavour during the Protestant ascendancy under Edward the Sixth, and had risen again during the submission to Rome under Mary. He had been a strong advocate of the marriage of Mary and Philip the Second of Spain, and had taken a leading part in the suppression of the Wyatt Rebellion against Mary. Later heads of the family had followed the same line: they belonged to that body of English Roman Catholic opinion which favoured Spain in feeling.

21

When in 1570 Pius the Fifth declared Elizabeth the First a usurper, excommunicated her, and released all her subjects from their oaths of allegiance to her, he put the Papists of England in a very difficult position. They could no longer communicate at Anglican altars without being excommunicated, and loyalty to their Queen had become treason to their church. Spain, which was now the chief military and imperialist instrument of the Papacy, and thus the defender of their cause, was also the enemy of their native country.

Thus the Gages became a family of conspirators. They must have believed that they were acting for their country's spiritual good against a régime which, while it had the temporary support of a blinded people, was not only wicked but illegitimate, and thus, in a sense, alien and un-English. Thomas's uncle, Robert Gage, had taken part in the plot of Anthony Babington, in which Spain had taken some interest, to assassinate Queen Elizabeth and replace her with Mary, Queen of Scots. He was captured in a barn and executed in 1586, two years before the Armada was defeated. Thomas's parents, John and Margaret, were almost executed for harbouring Jesuits. They escaped death through the intercession of Lord Howard of Effingham, a distant kinsman, who took, as a reward for this act of charity, their property near Croydon, Haling Park.

Thomas's immediate family were extraordinarily courageous and dedicated in their faith. His father, John, had the fault of his virtue, a rigidity of temperament which would not tolerate weakness. After her own close escape from execution, his mother, Margaret, was brave enough to burst through the crowd lining the street where her cousin, the poet and Jesuit Robert Southwell, was being led to his martyrdom, and to throw herself down before him, asking his blessing. Most of his brothers had distinguished themselves in some way, if only by their devotion to their church. Henry became a soldier in the service of Spain, and was to die fighting for Charles I, who had knighted him; George became a diplomat and a priest; William became a Jesuit. There were two sons by a second marriage: John became a secular priest, and Francis became head of Douai College, in France.

Thus Thomas had passed all his short life in an ambiency of intrigue and danger. His childhood had been spent in a house full of secret passages and hiding-places. He had been present when the solemnity of the Mass, celebrated before a few neighbours and servants, was interrupted by a confused noise of hooves outside the house, a rattle of steel and a loud, brutal pounding on the door. The priest would hastily take off his vestments, and run to a secret hiding place behind a sliding wall panel or the back of a false fireplace. The bread and wine would be whipped away; expressions of piety would change to ones of cheerful nonchalance, and the servants would be sent downstairs to delay the searchers with naïve and bumbling offers of help or honest words of outrage. Nobody could be trusted. One's neighbour, apparently firm in the faith, might suddenly turn around and denounce one; one's oldest and apparently most trustworthy servant might turn out to be a government informer. On the other hand, the agreeable and modest young man, newly arrived in the district, and overflowing with sentiments of loyalty to the régime in power, might reveal himself, at a propitious moment, as a Jesuit, newly arrived from Rome, Spain or France.

One could not even depend upon one's enemies. The anti-Romanist laws, which were very cruel when they were applied with full rigour, were sporadically enforced. By the time Gage was in his teens, there were very few executions, and those receiving lesser punishments seem to have been chosen almost at random, simply to inspire terror in the others.

The Roman Catholics were also in conflict among themselves. There was a virulent subterranean feud between the Jesuits, who were committed to active intrigue, and, if necessary, to assassination and rebellion, and the secular priests, who believed their duty lay simply in ministering to the dwindling body of their co-religionists. The government had nothing to fear from the latter: it often turned a blind eye to private Roman Catholic services, and sometimes intervened against over-zealous local magistrates. But when James the First attempted full toleration in 1603, demanding only that Romanists acknowledge the temporal sovereignty of the King rather than the Pope, hordes of Roman Catholics appeared as if from nowhere. The abolition of recusancy fines resulted in a shrinking of the congregations of many parish churches, and in certain neighbourhoods great numbers began to attend mass openly. Toleration was hastily withdrawn, and, it would seem, with good reason: in 1604 the Gunpowder Plot was discovered. Gage was then about two years old.

It was the policy of the Jesuits to enlist as many promising young Englishmen as they could. When Gage had been sent to school on the Continent—first, when he was only thirteen, at St Omer, and later at Valladolid—he had entered into a strange world which combined a rigid internal and external discipline and the teaching of self-sacrifice even to the point of martyrdom with a most poisonous and subtle form of intrigue. The English government, too, had its counter-intelligence agents in the Jesuit colleges of Europe.

Any personality would have been warped by such a childhood and adolescence; some personalities were terribly warped. It is not surprising that Thomas's thoughts, as he turned over Meléndez' proposition in his mind, were extraordinarily bitter.

He had less reason than most to love his father. He had just received a letter in which his father had informed him that he was disinheriting him because he had joined the Dominican Order. (Gage does not tell us under what circumstances he made the charge.) Not only had Thomas refused to fulfil his father's expressed desire that he become a Jesuit, John Gage said, but he had proved to be, in his affections, 'a deadly foe and enemy unto them'. Furthermore, he had added, Thomas must never expect to see his family again if he returned to England: the Jesuits would see that he was chased out of the country. When he thought of the secret influence exerted by the Jesuits in high places, even at Court, Gage could not underestimate the seriousness of this threat.

It is odd to find Gage, who had taken vows of poverty and belonged to a mendicant order, worrying about his inheritance. But Thomas had never had 'a sense of vocation', any more than those Franciscans of New Spain and Peru, mentioned in a papal declaration of 1578, who went to the New World to make themselves rich, and returned in secular dress. Gage denies it, but there is reason to believe that the factors which were influencing him towards an acceptance of Meléndez' proposition were quite secular in character: his prospects in England had been cut off; he had that deep curiosity about the wonders of America and Asia which then heated the imagination of almost every young man with an adventurous spirit; and he knew that a cunning priest, willing to cut a few moral corners, could do well in the Philippines. After his father died, he reasoned, he could return to England an independent and wealthy man.

That whole night he lay awake, and when the sun rose,

his mind was made up. He met Meléndez at breakfast, and agreed to join the mission. At lunch, he introduced Meléndez to his Irish friend, Tomás de León. And at dinner they met Friar Antonio Calvo, who greeted the pair with, as Gage depicts it, a most unctuous enthusiasm.

Calvo immediately set out to allay one of their fears about the ocean crossing. If they had had to depend on ship's stores, they would have had a very monotonous diet—biscuit, salt fish, salt meat, beans, bacon, cheese, onions and garlic, and what fish was caught during the voyage. But Calvo had a list of the foods he had laid in for his friars—'what varieties of fish and flesh, how many sheep, how many gammons of bacon, how many fat hens, how many hogs, how many barrels of white biscuit, how many jars of wine of Casalla, what store of rice, figs, olives, capers, raisins, lemons, sweet and sour oranges, pomegranates, comfits, preserves, conserves and all sorts of Portugal sweetmeats'. He spoke of his friars in the most flattering terms: he promised to make them all, when they arrived in Manila, Masters of Arts and of Divinity. He took out a heavy purse, and gave them coins to spend that day in Jerez—money to buy whatever they wished, with more than enough left over to carry them to Cadiz, the point of departure. And, to conclude, he spread out his hands, and bestowed a special benediction upon them.

The next morning they set out on the road to Puerto de Santa Maria, on the Bay of Cadiz: from there they would go to Cadiz, where they would meet Meléndez and the other friars. Since their luggage was being sent on by Calvo, they travelled light, riding on little asses 'like Spanish Dons'. As they passed through Jerez, they looked for the last time at its whitewashed houses with their narrow balconies and roof gardens. Then they were out of the town and in the country, where the great vineyards stretched for miles. They jogged on, down the quiet roads, until they came to the banks of the Guadalete, and that most beautiful and noble Carthusian convent which Andrés de Ribera had built some fifty years earlier, its façade ornate with pilasters and urns and the statues of saints.

The Guadalete was thought, in Gage's time, to be the Lethe of mythology, the river where souls drink, and forget the earth. So far as Gage was concerned, it was Spain he wanted to forget, and England as well.

By nightfall, they had reached the estuary of the Guadalete. They were in the town of Puerto de Santa Maria, looking out over the Bay of Cadiz. In the rapidly dimming light they could see, riding in the bay, the great vague forms of the galleons which were to take them to the New World.

They did not have much time, though, to gaze meditatively over the water. They were warriors of Christ, the valiant and humble vanguard of a Spain which, more than any other European country before or since, considered itself specially commissioned to establish a Christian Empire over the entire world. The spirit of the Crusades was still strong in Spain; here the secular and ornate glory of the Renaissance and early Baroque had not smothered the hard heraldic austerity of the Middle Ages, with its mysticism smelling of bread, blood and spring flowers, but had in a sense been swallowed up by it. The missionaries, toreros sallying forth to fight the bull of Hell in heathen lands, were being sainted while they were still alive.

Thus the town fathers of Puerto de Santa Maria had arranged that the streets through which they were to pass would be lined with cheering crowds. Admittedly—and the fact seems to sum up the way in which the realities of seventeenth-century Spanish life tended to betray the ideal—

a large number of the cheerers were galley slaves, commandeered for the occasion. But the cheers were loud for all that, and the trumpets were sounded as if for a procession of kings. When they had run this gauntlet of noisy veneration, one of the town notables, a certain Don Federico de Toledo, entertained them to supper, after which his gentlemen took them to a cloister of Franciscan mendicants, who washed their feet as the Lord had washed the feet of His apostles. They were then shown to bed.

The next morning, after a splendid breakfast at the Franciscan cloister, they were taken down to the shore. There they climbed into boats, and Don Federico's gentlemen took them to Cadiz, where they were to meet their fellow apostles. The Pope's Commissary, Friar Mateo de la Villa, entertained them at his own table, which was 'stored with fish and flesh'. 'There we continued in daily honour and estimation,' says Gage, 'enjoying the sights most pleasant which Cadiz both by sea and land could afford unto us, until the time of the fleet's departing.'

The pleasant sights of Cadiz! Cadiz was then, after Seville, the chief port for the American trade. In one sense it was richer than London or Amsterdam; in another, it was much poorer. It was rich, indeed, in the sense that a great deal of wealth passed through it. Spain, aspiring to be the perfect Christian state in an age of apostasy and venality, was, to its credit, quixotically anti-capitalist. It did not, as did many Protestant countries, attempt to foster the bourgeois way of life as if it were embodied virtue. Indeed, it regulated 'free enterprise' in much the same way that some cities control prostitution. Trade was, certainly, not respectable; those who sought the esteem of their fellows did not seek to make money, but to acquire a coat of arms. The trade of Spain was controlled by merchants resident in other

European states, many of them Jews who had been expelled from the country, and who traded through Spanish frontmen. Then, too, Spain was in continual debt: her European wars were expensive, and the bureaucracy was huge. Thus, while Cadiz was at any one time enormously rich, the town was simply a reservoir in which wealth was gathered and stored, so that it could be run out, through various conduits, many of which were secret and hidden, to the merchant towns of Italy and Northern Europe. It was the Genoese, with the exiled Marranos and the Huguenots of France, who profited most from the American trade.

Cadiz was one of the oldest commercial cities in the world: it had been founded by the Tyrians in 1100 B.C., on the site of an even older Tartessian city. Yet, to judge by its appearance, it might have been only a few hundred years old. For thousands of years, men had been pulling buildings down as fast as they put them up: there were no great edifices, and the cathedral, rebuilt after having been destroyed by Sir Francis Drake in 1596, twenty-nine years earlier, was unimpressive. (A few months after Gage left for America, Cadiz would be attacked by another English force, of nine thousand men, led by Lord Wimbledon.)

The town had its charms, though. It was famous for the acuity of its inhabitants, and the seductiveness of its dancing girls. Like Tyre, like Manhattan, it was built upon an island, and the population was crowded into a narrow space. Its colours were white and blue—the shell-white of its houses, so stark and bright in the sunlight that it hurt the eyes, and the pale, burning blue of the sky and sea. Its packed buildings, separated by narrow meandering streets, were as high as six stories. Behind the intricate iron-work of their balconies, red geraniums bloomed in pots. There were viewtowers, like tiny minarets, erected on their flat roofs: from these the inhabitants could gaze over the bay to see the first ships of the American fleet, or, perhaps, a flotilla of English pirates. This white, unadorned, baking-hot and crowded city must have produced then, as it does now, odd twinges of disquiet, as if one were out of Europe, and, indeed, out of time. Yet the waterfront would have brought one back to the contemporary realities which Gage's Spain was attempting to deny. There stood the great warehouses of the Genoese men of business—sugar merchants and international bankers closely connected with the financiers of Amsterdam.

It was now approaching the end of June, 1625. The Grand Apostle, Friar Mateo de la Villa, called his thirty Dominican missionaries together. They had thought he was himself prepared for a martyr's death, but he soon disabused them. He regretted that he would be unable to accompany them. His excuses were unconvincing: it seemed clear that, in spite of his words of encouragement, the Grand Apostle would sooner work in Spain for a bishopric than in Japan for a martyr's crown.

When he announced, further, that he had a commission from the Pope to nominate somebody in his place, and that the person in question would be Friar Antonio Calvo, he almost caused a mutiny. Indeed, two of the missionaries ran away. Calvo was an outrageous glutton—a fat bald old man whose white habit was spotted with bacon grease—and he more resembled an ageing scullion-boy than a Papal commissary. Some of the more cynical friars, though, did not object to his appointment. Calvo, they reasoned, was an old simpleton, and could easily be taken advantage of. Furthermore, since he was no lover of austerity, they would at least be sure of eating well.

It was under this slovenly and unattractive person, therefore, that their Apostolic Mission was to proceed—first to

Mexico, three thousand Spanish leagues from Spain, then, three thousand leagues further, to Manila, the viceregal capital of the Philippines.

II—*Sailing to America*

In the fleet which was to take the Dominicans to the New World there were forty-one ships, including eight galleons for protection against pirates. The ships had already been laden, under the supervision of an official of the House of Trade in Seville. Many of the passengers were on board: some of them, if this fleet was like the others, must have been prohibited immigrants—Protestants, Jews and newly-converted Jews, who were distrusted because they often practised their ancestral rites in private. These prohibited immigrants would have bought their way on board; once they were past the immigration officers of the Spanish colonies, their co-religionists would quietly help them to establish themselves.

There were many smuggled articles. The regulations demanded that all cargoes be registered at the House of Trade in Seville, but foreign merchants, forbidden to trade with the Indies, often put their goods on board by passing them up over the side. In addition, there was a contraband trade carried on by the religious orders: the monasteries and friaries near Seville and Cadiz were virtual smugglers' warehouses. Individual ecclesiastics and officers of the crown, who were not required to pay duty on their personal effects, because they were forbidden by law to engage in trade, often included large quantities of merchandise in their luggage: this would later be sold in America.

The official from the House of Trade had ascertained

'whether the ship is capable of making the trip, and the freight which it can take'. He had also checked the ships' manifests, but his inspection had been rather perfunctory by our standards. Each shipper had presented an itemized statement of his share of the cargo, and this had been accepted on face value. To have gone into the matter further would have been to cast doubt on the honour of the shippers, and this would have been outrageous. Nevertheless, the ships' manifests usually bore little relation to the cargo.

The ships themselves were vessels of from three hundred to two thousand tons, and they were too massive, as a rule, to defend themselves well against the small and mobile ships of pirates. Often the merchants put themselves in danger by their own greed: in the Philippine trade, for example, vessels were sometimes poorly armed, because the merchants resented relinquishing any of the precious lading space for the mounting of guns; it was not unheard of for the decks to be piled high with merchandise, while the guns were stored in the hold.

There was little space for the passengers. The cabins were hardly more than closets with lanterns hung before their doors. One had to guard, not only against shipwreck and piracy, but against an acute sense of confinement, and a restlessness which might bring passengers and crews to the edge of violence. Shipboard entertainments were many, but regulations were stern. Gambling, quarrelling and blasphemy were forbidden, as well as drunkenness and the carrying of slave women as concubines. There were places set aside for smoking, as a guard against fire, and here covered pipes and cigars in holders were permitted, but not cigarettes.

It is not surprising that there should have been violations of the rules relating to passengers' personal effects: each passenger was allowed only two small leather-covered trunks, writing materials, a mattress, a pair of bottle-cases for wine, and ten jars of 'chocolates, caramels, sweets, or anything else', which had to be stored under the benches in the cabins which served as beds. These delicacies were almost a necessity, the only relief from the extreme monotony of shipboard diet. There would be fish, of course, and at the beginning of the voyage, there would be fresh meat, fruits and vegetables, but these would not last long, unless one were travelling with a Calvo. On stormy days there would be only cold food and drink; it was too dangerous to light the ovens in bad weather. There were water-jars, some hung in the rigging, and others stored away above or below decks. A few large ships had cisterns. When it rained, water was collected in sloping mats which funnelled the downpour into jars, and sometimes heavy mats were hung in the rigging to collect moisture.

On the first of July in the afternoon, the admiral of the fleet, Don Carlos de Ybarra, gave the order, and the warning gun was fired. The passengers, soldiers and seamen prepared to board ship. Some of the less ardent missionaries were reluctant to leave Cadiz, where they had been a month at liberty. One of them, Friar Juan de Pacheco, who had fallen in love with a Franciscan sister, simply disappeared.

On the next day, the second of July, Thomas Gage received some disturbing news. Pablo de Londres, a 'crab-faced' old English friar in a cloister at San Lucar, near Cadiz, had forwarded to the Governor of Cadiz a letter from 'the Duke of Medina' (probably the very powerful Duke of Medina-Sidonia, whose palace was nineteen miles from Cadiz). It was an order that the Governor search out Thomas, and prevent his sailing. So far as we know, the Duke had no personal knowledge of Gage; he was simply acting on the King of Spain's decision that English Roman Catholics should not be allowed to go to the Indies, since they had a country of their own to convert. Perhaps the initiative had originally come from Friar Pablo, who had apparently troubled Gage before on this matter, sending him several letters urging him to go to England. Friar Pablo had also forwarded, this time to Gage, a letter from the Castilian Provincial of the Dominicans, which made offers of preferment if Gage would forget about the Philippines, and join him in Castile. The Provincial had some knowledge of Gage's family, at least. Under the alias of Friar Diego de la Fuente, he had recently been secretary to the Spanish ambassador to England; thus he knew the situation of English Romanists. But more than that, he had been one of the go-betweens in the secret negotiations aimed at effecting a match between the then Prince of Wales, soon to be Charles the First, and the Infanta Maria of Spain. Thomas's brother, George, had been one of the go-betweens on the English side.

Thomas had no desire, though, to return to England or to go to Castile. Nor did Calvo wish to lose a missionary the day before departure. When the Governor of Cadiz came to Calvo to inquire about Gage, the Englishman had disappeared. He had been rowed to the ship on which the Dominicans were sailing, and hidden in a biscuit-barrel. Later, when all the friars had boarded, the Governor came to the ship; but when he asked if there was an Englishman among them, Calvo resolutely denied it. Jokes about this little deception were common, thereafter, among the company of apostles.

The time of departure had come. The remaining passengers were rowed out in cock-boats to the ship. One by one they stepped nervously on to the rungs of the rope-ladder, and climbed up the side.

34

Then the sails were hoisted, the anchors hauled in, and amid shouts, the flapping of canvas, and the running to and fro of seamen, the ships began to move out. The passengers, reluctant to go below to their tiny cabins, stood on deck staring at the shore, and nerving themselves for two months of danger, deprivation and boredom. 'Adios! Adios!' they shouted at the watchers on the shore, and the watchers cried back 'Buen viaje! Buen viaje!' Some of the friars wished they were ashore again; others hung over the side, aimlessly feeding the fish with bits of cake and pastry given them by the sisters; others stared about them, marvelling at the forty great ships, which stood, on the wide lawns of the water, like palaces and churches whose towers and spires were masts webbed with rigging and hung with sails. The destinations of the thirty-three merchant vessels were, to them, mere names—two for Puerto Rico, three for Santo Domingo, two for Jamaica, one for Margarita, two for Havana, three for Cartagena, two for Campeche, two for Honduras and Trujillo, and sixteen for Vera Cruz. In their holds were wines, figs, raisins, olives, coarse woollens, linen, iron and quicksilver for the silver mines of Zacatecas.

Some of the passengers were most distinguished. The year before there had been a violent quarrel between the Viceroy of Mexico, the Count de Gelvés and the Mexican Archbishop. The public had become involved; there had been riots, and the Viceroy had had to take refuge in a monastery. The King had appointed a new viceroy, the Marqués de Serralvo; he and his wife, the vicereine, were in the *San Andrés*. With them was Don Martín de Carrillo, a priest from the Inquisition at Valladolid, commissioned to inquire into the causes of the mutiny. In the *Santa Gertrudis* was the new president of Manila, as well as thirty Jesuits, who had managed to take passage on the same ship (Gage says) so that they might ingratiate themselves with him, 'for this cunning generation studies purposely how to ingratiate themselves with kings, princes, great men, rulers and commanders'.

In the *Nuestra Señora de Regla*, there were thirty Mercedarian friars bound for Mexico. Gage and the remaining twenty-seven Dominican missionaries to the Philippines were in the *San Antonio*.

The great fleet cleared the Bay of Cadiz, and, over calm seas, sailed to the Canaries. This was where the galleons, having escorted the merchant vessels through the pirate-infested coastal seas, were to leave them. It was an occasion for high ceremony, and the small boats passed and repassed from ship to ship. The Admiral of the Fleet entertained the Admiral of the Galleons at dinner, a ceremony duplicated, on a lower level of rank, among the captains and officers of the other ships. The passengers hastily finished their letters, which would be taken back in the galleons to be posted in Spain. Then, the dinners and leavetakings over, the Admiral of the Galleons was rowed back to his ship, the guns were fired, and the galleons, their timbers and cordage creaking, pulled away from the merchant ships.

Another tie with Spain had been severed, and the departure of the galleons had much diminished the zeal of some of the missionaries. These tried to persuade Calvo to let them return; but that, of course, was impossible. There was no turning back. Many would never see Spain again.

Yet it was a calm and easy voyage, and the boredom of the long crossing was alleviated by shipboard entertainments. On the last day of July—the day of their patron saint, Ignatius—the Jesuits made the *Santa Gertrudis* as gay as a ship in a tapestry. They trimmed it around with white linen: they hoisted portraits of Ignatius, and flags and banners bearing the arms of the Jesuits. All night there were fire-crackers, and the guns of the ship were fired; trumpets and hymns could be heard across the black water, and the masts and ropes were hung with gently-glowing paper lanterns, which outlined them in beads of light. The next day the Jesuits could be seen moving in procession round the deck of the *Santa Gertrudis*, singing hymns in praise of their patron.

On the fourth of August, St Dominic's day, the Dominicans on the *San Antonio* strove to outdo the Jesuits. Again there were fireworks, gun-fire, and singing by day and night. That day the Dominicans asked all the Jesuits, along with the new President of Manila and the captain of the *Santa Gertrudis*, to dinner on board the *San Antonio*. In the afternoon, after dinner, some of the soldiers, passengers and younger friars acted one of the plays of Lope de Vega, who was then at the peak of his extraordinary career. Gage thought it was as well acted upon the *San Antonio* as it might have been at the Court of Madrid, but when one considers the elaborate nature of Spanish court theatre, it is clear that this statement is an affectionate exaggeration.

On the twentieth of August, 1625, about seven weeks after they had left Cadiz, they sighted their first land. We cannot now identify this island, which the Spaniards then called Deseada. Then there was another island called Marie Galante: Columbus had named it after one of his ships. They passed Dominica, so named because Columbus had discovered it, 132 years earlier, on a Sunday. They were in the Caribbean, in those days still a Spanish sea. Islands were always on the horizon, visible as mere bumps or thickenings of the horizon line. Eventually they came to Guadeloupe.

III—*Guadeloupe*

COLUMBUS had first discovered Guadeloupe in 1493, and in doing so had discovered a predecessor, or a memento of one. In a Carib village, twenty or thirty palm-thatched huts set around a cleared space which acted as the village square, his men had found an iron cooking-pot and the stern-post of a large vessel. They did not recognize the stern-post and the Caribs did not work iron. The name and nation of this particular predecessor of Columbus has remained a mystery. It is possible that these two articles were salvaged from a floating derelict, the wreck of some European vessel which, caught in the trade-winds, had drifted across the Atlantic from Europe or Africa.

When Columbus first visited the island, he found the natives using human skulls as household utensils; there were human limbs curing in the rafters, and human flesh boiling in the pots, along with that of geese and parrots. These natives were the fierce Caribs, who, with the peaceable Arawaks, then inhabited the entire Caribbean—a race of Cains living beside a race of Abels. By Gage's time, however, the Caribs were already rather clownish and pathetic. They had come to depend on the yearly visit of the *flota* as much as the merchants of Vera Cruz. The old Caribbean economy had fallen into ruin: now both Caribs and Arawaks busied themselves, when they felt like working, in preparing sugar-cane, plantains and cured tortoise-meat, which they would give to the Spaniards in exchange for cloth and iron knives. They had become seedy and nondescript, collectors of cultural cast-offs. Their canoes were decorated with the coats-of-arms of the nations who visited them—the Spaniards, English, French and Dutch.

Their canoes slid against the steep-sided ships, and they clambered aboard, figures naked or almost naked, with painted faces, long hanging hair, and thin nose-plates which resembled, Gage notes contemptuously, so many hog-rings. They plucked the Spaniards' sleeves, and fawned on them, begging for wine in sign-language. Soon they were rolling drunk on the deck of the ship.

After the Spaniards had amused themselves, for a while, by watching the Indians, the cock-boat was lowered, so that those who wished could enjoy the pleasures of the island. Some went simply to set foot on dry land, any land; some went to bathe themselves, and to wash their musty and ill-smelling clothes; some went, no doubt, in search of women. Those who disembarked were seamen and lay passengers; a few did not return that night, but slept on shore among the Indians.

The friars disembarked the next morning. Leaving their soiled clothing with some Spaniards whom they had hired as laundrymen, they wandered along the beach alone, or in small groups. Everywhere they were accosted by Indians, who, with the most servile respect, offered them the fruits of the island, and begged trifles in exchange—pins or gloves.

The Indians coaxed the friars to come to their village, so 'we ventured', Gage says, 'to go to some of their houses which stood by a pleasant river, and were by them kindly entertained, eating of their fish, and wild deer's flesh.'

About noon, as Gage and a few companions were walking in the mountains, they came across some of the Jesuits of the *Santa Gertrudis*, engaged in serious conversation with a half-naked mulatto. Gage, when he had gone up to the group, learned from the ensuing conversation that the man was, or had been, a Christian. His name was Luis, and he spoke perfect Spanish. Apparently he had been the personal slave of a gentleman bound for America; but had deserted the ship in Guadeloupe, having found that he preferred the company of Indians to the service of Spaniards. He had hidden in the forest until the ship had gone, and then had emerged, giving the Indians, as presents, certain goods which he had stolen from his master. He had been among the Indians some twelve years: he spoke their language and was married, with three children.

Gage and his Dominican companions joined the Jesuits, who were engaged in a relentless assault on the man's conscience. How could he have forsaken the way of Christ, prostrating himself before rude representations of the spirits of the mountains, waters and forests? How could he have given up the God who had revealed Himself in the full glory of His human nature for a vague sky-spirit—immortal and omnipotent, it is true, but quite uninterested in the affairs of men? Luis, though he had lived as a pagan for twelve years, began to weep. The Gospel is strong. He would gladly go with them, he said, but he could not leave his wife and children, whom he loved. Bring them with you, the Spaniards replied, and their souls will be saved. Furthermore, they added, Luis would be freed, and the Church would support him until he was able to earn a reasonable living. Luis was listening with great attention, until some Indians passed by. When they saw their Luis in earnest conversation with the missionaries, they began to talk angrily among themselves. At this, Luis drew away: it was dangerous, he said, for him to talk to the missionaries; the Indians might kill him to prevent the Spaniards taking him from the island, and, indeed, they would probably turn on the Spaniards.

You have nothing to worry about, said the Spaniards, our

ship has soldiers, small arms and ordnance enough to protect us all. Then they told Luis to bring his wife and children to that place on the shore where the Spaniards were drying their clothes: there would be a boat there to take them on board ship. Luis finally agreed, saying that he would entice his wife and children to the beach with the story that he was going down to trade with the Spaniards. Some of the Jesuits, he said, should be standing by the boat.

The Jesuits went to the shore, to tell the Admiral of their promise to Luis, and to arrange that a cock-boat should be ready as agreed. By now Gage and most of the friars were returning to the ship. When they were on board, a discussion began. Many, motivated either by apostolic zeal or the depressing thought of the many leagues they had yet to travel, wanted to stay on Guadeloupe. Were not the Indians a loving and tractable people? In any case, they said, they would not be in much danger, since the Spanish fleet arrived once a year, and its soldiers would certainly punish the natives if they were mistreated. And after all, added the most zealous among them, the worst that could happen to one would be to find a grave in the belly of a Carib. Had they not come out of Spain to seek the crown of martyrdom?

So they talked, looking at the rich green shore of Guadeloupe, which was still dotted with the small figures of those Spaniards who had not yet returned to the ship. A few black-robed Jesuits were standing near a beached cock-boat, trying not to look as if they were waiting for somebody. Then, inexplicably, everybody began to run towards the water. Many of them were half-naked, but they had left their clothes drying in the sun. The Spaniards were pushing off all the boats, and clambering into them in such haste that they were foundering, or shipping water in dangerous quantities. Some of the women passengers were throwing themselves shrieking into the sea. Arrows were flying out of the jungle like clouds of gnats.

The ship's cannons were fired, and a company of armed soldiers took to the boats and rowed to the shore. When they reached the land, there were no more arrows flying from the trees, and the dead and wounded were scattered about the shore, rocking back and forth in the shallow water near the beach, or floating farther out. Two Jesuits had been killed and ten wounded; three passengers were missing. Fifteen persons had drowned in the attempt to escape. Among the wounded was one Friar Juan de la Cueva, who, some short time before, had been trying to persuade Gage to stay on shore a little while longer. He had an arrow in his shoulder.

Luis had not turned up. It was assumed that he had told the Caribs of the Jesuits' plan to steal him away, or that the Caribs, seeing him in conversation with them, had made him confess it. But the first explanation seemed more probable to Gage: Luis had told the Jesuits he would know them by their black coats, and it was observed that most of the arrows were directed at the Jesuits, five of whom were struck in slightly more than fifteen minutes.

All that night the soldiers kept watch along the shore. An armed guard accompanied those who went to the river to fetch water; and muskets were fired at irregular intervals, both to frighten the Indians, and to attract the attention of the three passengers who were missing in the jungle. But the Indians had vanished, and so, it seemed, had the three passengers. A watch was mounted on board the ships and few slept, for fear the Indians might attack in their canoes. Friar Juan de la Cueva lay sleepless and in agony, the wound in his shoulder festering.

At noon, with a good breeze, they hoisted the sails, and left Guadeloupe.

Most of the friars now began to lose their desire for martyrdom, fed by books of saints' lives and monastery frescoes. It was the first time, doubtless, that many of them had seen death by violence. Friar Juan de la Cueva was in continual pain, and his body was swelling: the arrow, it was clear, had been poisoned. On the twenty-second of August, four days out from Guadeloupe, he died.

'His burial', says Gage, 'was as solemnly performed as could be at sea. His grave being the whole ocean, he had weighty stones hung at his feet, two more to his shoulders, and one to his breast; and then the superstitious Romish dirge and requiem being sung for his soul, his corpse being held out to the sea on the ship side with ropes ready to let him fall, all the ship crying out three times, *Buen viaje, a good voyage*, to his soul chiefly, and also to his corpse ready to travel to the deep to feed the whales: at the first cry all the ordnance were shot off, the ropes on a sudden loosed, and Juan de la Cueva with the weight of heavy stones plunged deep into the sea, whom no mortal eyes ever more beheld. The like we saw performed in the ship of *Santa Gertrudis* to another Jesuit, one of the three who had been dangerously wounded by the Indians of Guadeloupe; which likewise died like our friar, his body being swelled as with poison.'

The friars were now discouraged and frightened, and Calvo tried to comfort them. The natives of the Philippines, he said, were not like those of Guadeloupe. Most of them were Christians already, and treated the priests as if they were gods; and those who were pagans stood in awe of the soldiers.

They passed Puerto Rico, and then the great island of Santo Domingo or Hispaniola, long settled by the Spaniards. Now many of the ships began to leave the fleet, heading for ports in the Caribbean or Central America. Only the sixteen ships of the Mexican fleet were left.

In the Gulf of Mexico they were becalmed, and for a week

the ships lay, barely moving, in the blue and tepid water. The friars passed the time angling for the little golden fish known to the Spaniards as *dorados*. But the heat was unbearable: the unpitying sun glared on the decks and pitchy sides of the ships, and their sweat ran continually. The evenings and nights were only slightly more comfortable. Nobody could sleep in the cabins. They were, after all, as tiny as the fo'c'sle of a modern tug boat: the ceilings were too low for standing; the beds were only little benches attached to the sides of the ship, with a few cushions for comfort; they smelled of tar and unwashed bodies, and were hung with musty clothes, water-jars and miscellaneous gear. At night the friars, stripped to their shirts, walked, sat or lay on the deck. The mariners washed frequently to cool off; some of them swam by the sides of the ships.

'The nearer we come to the mainland,' says Gage, 'the sea abounds with a monstrous fish, called by the Spaniards *tiburón*.' He had seen one caught with an iron trident: 'a most monstrous creature, twelve ells long at least'. Since these sharks stayed away from the ships, one could swim by the sides without much danger. But one of the mariners of the *San Francisco* was something of an exhibitionist: he began to swim from his ship to another, where he had friends. A shark pulled him three times under the water, taking off a leg, an arm and part of a shoulder. By the time they had lowered a boat, he was already dead. They picked up the bleeding trunk, and buried it as they had Friar Juan de la Cueva.

Three days later, the wind rose, and they moved out of the calm.

IV—*Arrival in Mexico*

It was seven o'clock, on a Monday morning, and one of the
friars was saying Mass. Then a voice cried out *Tierra, tierra.*
The communicants rose from their knees to see the American
mainland.

At about ten that morning, they could see the coast, and
they were running towards it under full sail. Friar Calvo was
slaughtering some of his best fowls. Their anguished and
strangled clucking mingled with the chatter of the passengers.

The harbour of San Juan de Ullua, which was also called
Vera Cruz after a now-abandoned port to the south, was
difficult to enter. There were a number of reefs and banks of
shingles: one of these, the Arrecife de la Gallega, which lay
about a quarter of a mile from the coast, was high enough to
shelter the harbour from the dangerous northerlies. On this
reef a great fort had been built, to further shelter the harbour
from pirates, and beyond it, in the harbour, flags and buoys
marked scattered rocks. The town was built on the shore.

It was September, and the season of the northerlies: there
was thus some danger of being driven on to the rocks. The
pilots, the navigating officers of the ships, met in council, and
they decided that, since they would have the help of the
harbour pilots the next morning, they would lower all but
their middle sails, and approach the shore slowly during the
rest of that day and night. That night, a double watch was
mounted.

Just before midnight, the wind turned to the north. This
change, even though the wind was not at all boisterous,

45

Travels of Thomas Gage in Mexico and Guatemala (1625-37)

85°

80°

20°

C a r i b b e a n   S e a

Trujillo

15°

O N D U R A S

Comayagua

NICARAGUA

El Viejo
Realejo

eón

Lake
Nicaragua

Granada

Salinas
Bay

Nicoya

Rio Desaguadero
Rio Sueré

10°

Cartago

Portobello

COSTA RICA

Panama

P A N A M A

through Central America to Portobello (1637)

created a mild panic. The friars lit candles, and all night they sang hymns and litanies, and offered up prayers to the Virgin. 'Towards the dawning of the day', says Gage, 'our wonted gale' [presumably it was an easterly wind] 'began to blow again.'

At about eight in the morning, they came in sight of the Gallega Reef, with its fort, church and hospital. The houses of Vera Cruz lay beyond. They signalled for boats; and as the boats were launched from the shore and moved towards them, the musicians on the ships began to play their oboes and trumpets, the guns were fired, and the guns on shore replied.

Cautiously the ships manoeuvred round the fort and into the shadow of its great wall, which rose, green with seaweed, from the sea; the stern anchors were run out, and the head-ropes secured to the huge bronze rings in the wall.

If Gage had been standing on the poopdeck, looking over the stern of the ship, he would have seen, among the craft putting out from the shore, the boats of the Crown customs officers and inspectors of the Holy Office. Mexican customs officials and immigration officers may have been, by modern standards, relatively unsuccessful in their attempts to keep out smuggled goods and subversive persons; but they did try.

The town of Vera Cruz, so famous for its riches, was in fact ugly and down-at-heel. The town-site, surrounded by the coarse lush vegetation of the coastal jungle, was a stretch of dirty sand broken by tiny oozing streams and pitted with bogs, 'which, with the great heats that are there, cause it to be a very unhealthy place'. Vera Cruz did not have the wharves of a modern port, since ships anchored by the fort. A simple mole stuck out into the water, with a Customs House at its landward end. The town itself was a straggling assemblage of crudely-constructed buildings, which were, though larger, hardly more substantial than booths at a fair. Indeed, that is what they were: like Acapulco, and Portobello (which Gage would visit later), Vera Cruz was the setting of a great annual market. The Spanish *flota* had much in common with the Asian or medieval European caravan, and, like the caravan, disposed of its goods at a fair. The rich merchants met the fleet at Vera Cruz; there they collected the goods consigned to them or haggled over goods sent for resale in Mexico or the Far East; and when the fair was over, they left. Their homes were in such inland towns as Jalapa: men of position, able to make a choice, would hardly live in such a hot, dank, disease-ridden town as Vera Cruz. The permanent residents were poor and ignorant—peasants, fishermen, beach-combers. Gage could have seen them on the beach, gazing out at the ships: Negroes, Indians and poor whites, almost naked or dressed in rags. Here and there were lumbering ox-carts, and donkeys half-hidden beneath loads of faggots.

But now there were a number of splendid personages on shore: wealthy merchants, pompous government officials, and priests. The Inquisitors and customs officials, already aboard the ship and checking the passenger lists and ships' manifests, had their own ominous authority.

When the friars and Jesuits reached the shore, some of them kissed the ground, sanctified by the labours of the first missionaries, and others knelt to offer up prayers to the Virgin and the saints. They then went to stand with their fellows in the places appointed to their respective orders.

'In the meantime all the cannon playing both from ships and castle, landed the Viceroy and his lady and all his train accompanied with Don Martin de Carrillo the Visitor-General for the strife between the Count of Gelves, the last Viceroy, and the Archbishop of Mexico. The great Don and his lady being placed under a canopy of state, began the *Te Deum* to be sung with much variety of musical instruments, all marching in procession to the Cathedral, where with many lights of burning lamps, torches, and wax candles, was to the view of all set upon the high altar their God of bread; to whom all knees were bowed, a prayer of thanksgiving sung, holy water by a priest sprinkled upon all the people, and lastly a Mass with three priests solemnly celebrated. This being ended, the Viceroy was attended on by the Chief High Justice, named *Alcalde Mayor*, by the officers of the town, some judges sent from Mexico to that purpose, and all the soldiers of the ships and town unto his lodgings. The friars likewise in procession with their cross before them were conducted to their several cloisters.'

V—*Vera Cruz*

GAGE and the other Dominicans—Friar Calvo at their head —were marched to the Priory of St Dominic. The Prior welcomed each of them with a cup of chocolate and some sweetmeats; this was followed by a sumptuous dinner of capons, turkey cocks and chickens—an example, he said, of the abundance of the country. After dinner he entertained them with songs, accompanying himself on the guitar.

Gage professes himself to have been more shocked than pleased. The Prior particularly enraged him. He was not a grave and grey-headed man, such as one would expect to find governing young and wanton friars; rather, he was a gallant young spark, feather-headed and shallow of temperament, who had purchased his position from his Provincial for a thousand ducats. His private chamber contained only a few dozen decayed volumes of theology, and they were covered with dust and cobwebs; but his guitar was hung on the wall within easy reach. Round about the chamber were hung many pictures and tapestries in the style of the country, made of cotton or the feather-work of Michoacán; his tables had covers of silk and his cupboards were full of dishes and cups from China, all of which, Gage tells us (he had a sweet tooth, and noticed such things), were filled with comfits. His conversation was neither pious nor edifying. He boasted a good deal—about his birth, his cleverness, the fondness his Provincial had for him, the love borne him by the wives of the rich merchants, and his great skill in music. When he sang, his voice quivered artfully and lasciviously, and the song was one he had composed in praise of 'some lovely Amaryllis'. Gage, munching savagely on sweetmeats flavoured with musk and civet, noted it all for future reference.

Eventually the coxcombical Prior ran out of songs and self-praise. Gage and the other friars decided, since they would be there for only a day and a half, to take a turn about the town. It took them only an afternoon to see all there was to see.

'Of the buildings,' Gage says, 'little we observed, for they [are] all, both houses, churches, and cloisters, built with boards and timber, the walls of the richest man's house being made but of boards, which with the impetuous winds from the north hath been cause that many times the town hath been for the most part of it burnt down to the ground.'

The population of Vera Cruz was, in Gage's time, about three thousand, and there were among them (though probably not permanently resident in the port) 'some very rich merchants, some worth two hundred, some three hundred, and some four hundred thousand ducats'. A few of the houses, like those of Cadiz, had watch-towers, so that the nervous money-bags who owned them could look out to sea, and be warned of the approach of English or Dutch pirates. Others were connected by underground passages. The townspeople were never free from the fear of attack by privateers or pirates, since it was here that much of the silver and gold of the Indies, and many of the rare goods of China and South-east Asia awaited trans-shipment to Spain. But the town itself was open: Vera Cruz trusted for its defence to the difficult harbour entrance, and the fort on the Arrecife de la Gallega.

That night, when the friars were sleeping, a strong north wind blew up. The rough boards of the Priory began to rattle together, and the entire building was tottering and shaking so much that the newly-arrived Dominicans, fearing its imminent collapse, ran barefoot into the dirty yard. The resident friars laughed at them: they never slept easier, they said, than when the wind was blowing; it kept raiders away, at least. But in the morning they found that the wind had snapped the cables of one of the ships in which they had crossed the Atlantic, and driven it out to sea.

They had no desire to stay in the unhealthy little port, and they were not disappointed when Calvo announced that they were moving inland the next morning. Thirty mules, brought from Mexico City six days earlier, were already waiting for them. Calvo, who seems to have been a conscientious and thrifty quartermaster, oversaw the repacking of the provisions that were left over from the voyage—wine, biscuits, bacon, salt beef, twelve live hens and three sheep. That evening, they went to the church to see a comedy which the town had prepared for the entertainment of the Viceroy, and the next morning they set out for Mexico City.

VI—*From Vera Cruz to Mexico City*

IN the journey from Vera Cruz to Mexico City, Gage was for the first time treated in the manner Meléndez had led him to expect. The priests and friars were entertained as if they were visiting gods, or Oriental despots at the very least, that is, they were greeted with that elaborate ceremonial humility with which the Mexican peoples had once approached the lords and high priests of the Aztecs. The first town they came to was Old Vera Cruz, now a small Indian village. Twenty of the important villagers met them on horseback: they gave each of the friars a nosegay of flowers, and rode a bow-shot ahead of them until they were met by the chief party from the village—trumpeters, choristers, and heads of the various saints' sodalities.

The procession moved to the chief market-place of the town, and after the municipal officers had knelt and kissed the hands of the friars one by one, they rose to deliver elaborate and interminable speeches of welcome, calling them the Apostles of Jesus Christ, saying they honoured them as if they were gods on earth, and thanking them for having crossed the sea to save their souls. While they were listening, the friars drank chocolate. The spokesman for the friars responded by saying that they indeed cared for nothing but saving the souls of the Indians, and that it was for this they had faced unimaginable dangers by land and sea.

This exchange of florid civilities went on for about an hour. Then the earthly gods took their departure, after having given the village notables some beads, medals, brass crosses and religious relics from Spain, and granted everyone in the village an indulgence of forty years. The market-place was full of kneeling Indians, and the friars, as they departed on their mules, lifted their hands, scattering blessings on their bowed heads.

The trumpeters and choristers, lustily blowing and singing, accompanied them a mile out of town, then left them in order to return to their village. The friars went on through the fertile and varied countryside, which—with its great canyons and tree-carpeted barrancas, its rich pastures, corn-fields and sugar-plantations climbing up the sides of steep hills, its valleys where the vegetation proliferated with jungle-like fecundity, its mountain peaks marching upwards to the interior—resembled a Romantic painter's dream of the Garden of Eden. Yet everywhere Gage found evidence of luxury, extortion and venality.

In the town of Jalapa they stayed in a huge Franciscan convent, where six friars were living on the revenues, ade-quate to support twenty men in excellent style, of a huge monastic estate. The rules of their order demanded that they wear sackcloth and shirts of coarse wool, and that they go bare-legged, shod with wood or hemp; but these friars wore beneath their habits (which they sometimes tucked up to the waist, the better to display such splendour), shoes of fine Cordovan leather, fine silk stockings, drawers with three inches of lace at the knee, holland shirts, and doublets quilted with silk. They were fond of gambling, and acquainted with gamblers' oaths. Each, no doubt, had his own way of re-conciling such luxury and greed with the oaths he had taken. One, whom Gage observed in a game of primera, jokingly used the end of one sleeve to sweep his winnings into the other, explaining that the rules of his order did not allow him to touch money.

54

There is no doubt that the worldly opulence of the Mexican church was well in excess of the splendours necessary to ritual and the income necessary to use: we must not take Gage's criticism as a simple expression of prejudice. As early as 1556, the Archbishop of Mexico, himself a Dominican, had complained of convents, intended to accommodate only two or three friars, which 'would more than suffice for Valladolid'. The labour, and often the monetary costs, of construction and upkeep were supplied by the Indians.

They passed through La Rinconada, an inn in a low hot valley where they were tormented by gnats, and through Segura, now called Tepeaca. It was in Segura that Gage first tasted the zapote, whose sweet brown or scarlet-purple flesh tastes more like a man-made confection than a fruit. They came to Tlaxcala, whose inhabitants, joining with Cortés against their traditional enemies, the Aztecs, had made the Conquest possible. In his book, Gage, who seems to have made up for his gluttony by his vigorous disapproval of the pleasures of art, looks back with distaste to the music he heard in the church attached to the Franciscan cloister of Ocotelulco, one of the quarters of Tlaxcala. Here there were some fifty Indian singers, organists and instrumentalists, who, Gage says, 'set out the Mass with a very sweet and harmonious music, and delight the fancy and senses, while the spirit is sad and dull as little acquainted with God, who will be worshipped in spirit and in truth'.

From Tlaxcala they went to Puebla, then, as now, one of the most beautiful cities of America. Built on the site of the insignificant Aztec village of Cuetlaxcoapán, it was essentially a colonial foundation, with no Indian past of importance. Indeed, the legend of its foundation (Puebla is full of legends of the colonial period) states that the site was shown to its founder in a dream. Fray Julián Garcés, the story goes, saw

55

two angels holding a string and a measuring rod over some land at the foot of Popocatépetl: this is why the city subsequently built on the site was called Puebla de los Angeles, the City of the Angels. Gage's account, more prosaic, merely says that the city was built in 1530, by order of the Viceroy. It has been called, from its more than sixty churches, 'the Rome of America': in Gage's time, too, it was notable for its many ecclesiastical buildings. The noble cathedral, based on designs by Juan de Herrera, the architect of the Escurial, was then in construction; it would be finished in 1649, when Gage was back in England.

'This city is now a bishop's see, whose yearly revenues since the cutting off from it Jalapa de la Vera Cruz are yet worth above twenty thousand ducats. By reason of the good and wholesome air it daily increaseth with inhabitants, who resort from many other places to live there; but especially the year 1634, when Mexico was like to be drowned with the inundation of the lake, thousands left it, and came with all their goods and families to this City of the Angels, which now is thought to consist of ten thousand inhabitants. That which maketh it most famous is the cloth which is made in it, and is sent far and near, and judged now to be as good as the cloth of Segovia, which is the best that is made in Spain, but now is not so much esteemed of nor sent so much from Spain to America by reason of the abundance of fine cloth which is made in this City of Angels. The felts likewise that are made are the best of all that country; there is also a glass house, which is there a rarity, none other being as yet known in those parts. But the mint house that is in it, where is coined half the silver that cometh from Zacatecas, makes it the second to Mexico; and it is thought that in time it will be as great and populous as Mexico. Without it there are many gardens, which store the markets with provision of salads, the soil abounds with wheat, and with sugar farms, among the which not far from this city there is one so great and populous,

56

(belonging to the Dominican friars of Mexico) that for the work only belonging unto it, it maintained in my time above two hundred blackamoor slaves, men and women besides their little children.'

What Gage does not tell us is that Puebla had achieved its reputation as a cloth town at the price of much human suffering. The mills, in which Indians, Chinese, Filipinos and Africans worked along with convicts serving their sentences, were quite as bad as those of early nineteenth-century England, and were thus, in a sense, 'progressive'. Hours were cruelly long, and the workers, many of whom were children of six or seven years old, were often locked in the factories overnight. It is true that the labour laws of the Spanish Empire, which were comparatively just, forbade such practices; but social justice was already coming to be considered a reactionary concept: the trend was towards unrestricted free enterprise, and it was becoming more and more difficult to enforce laws which the mercantile and manufacturing classes considered punitive.

Puebla was thus an important manufacturing and business town, whose substantial citizens would no doubt have approved the following two stanzas from *La Grandeza Mexicana*, by the former Abbot of Jamaica, and at that time Bishop of Puerto Rico, Bernardo de Balbuena—one of the first to attempt to make poetry out of the odious paradoxes of enlightened self-interest—

> *There is no place where greed may not be found.*
> *Each occupation has its dividend.*
> *Cupidity makes the whole world go round,*
>
> *And all things does he strengthen and defend.*
> *He is the sun who vivifies the ground,*
> *And governs the beginning and the end.*

(That very year, though, the progressive Bishop was to suffer at the hands of the chief exponents of free enterprise in that age: in 1625, the Dutch occupied San Juan de Puerto Rico, and burned down his house.)

From Puebla they went to Huejotzingo. Here Gage was profoundly shocked to discover that the Franciscans were teaching the Indian children to dance to the guitar. The friars were entertained till midnight by these children, who sang Spanish and Indian tunes, 'capering and dancing with their castanets, or knockers, on their fingers'.

Then, from Huejotzingo, they climbed the mountains around Mexico, and looked down on that famous valley, which had been civilized almost as long as Spain. Here there had stood the great imperial city of Teotihuacan, a city of eight square miles, larger than Imperial Rome. Then had come the empires of the Toltecs, the Chichimecs, and the Aztecs—all centred in this valley. Finally, new Spanish-speaking cities and a Baroque Christian culture had obliterated the cruel society of the Aztecs, leaving only a sullen folk-culture like that of the peasants of the outlying parts of Europe.

On the third day of October, 1625, they entered the city. But they passed through it, since they were on their way to the Dominican establishment among the gardens near Chapultepec, known as San Jacinto. Gage was to stay there five months.

VII—*The City of Mexico*

THE house at San Jacinto was a beautiful place. Its grounds, in which there were grape arbours and shady walks under the orange and lemon trees, covered fifteen acres. All the fruits of Mexico were to be found there—pomegranate, fig, plantain, zapote and pineapple. Discipline was minimal, and life was undemanding. There was good reason for this apparent laxity. The friars had to stay in Mexico for a few months, if for no other reason than that the fleet did not sail from Acapulco till February. Travel was hard in those days, and they needed a rest between the long journey from Spain to Mexico City, and the much longer journey from Mexico City to the Philippines. Furthermore, since the life of even an average Mexican religious was much freer and more luxurious than that any of the Spanish friars had been used to, many of them would have been tempted, had they been condemned to five months of austerity, to desert the Philippine mission and take refuge in a Mexican religious community. Thus, in the house at San Jacinto, which was under the control of the Dominican superior in the Philippines, they were consciously pampered.

Living under this régime of luxury, Gage's appetite seems to have increased. Every Monday morning, each of the friars was brought half a dozen boxes of conserves of quinces, and other sugared fruits, as well as a good supply of biscuits. Gage found that he was continually nibbling between meals, and he asked a physician to explain this oddity. The physician, who seems to have been of a type Molière (had he not been only three years old at the time) would have recognized, replied that while Mexican meat looked as good as Spanish, it was far inferior because the pasture was drier and scantier. Secondly, he said, 'the climate of those parts had this effect, to produce a fair show but little matter of substance', thus both flesh and fruits 'have little inward virtue or nourishment at all in them'. Gage draws a moral from this: 'I have heard reported much among the Spaniards to have been the answer of our Queen Elizabeth of England to some that presented unto her of the fruits of America, that surely where those fruits grew, the women were light, and all the people hollow and false-hearted.'

Since San Jacinto was only two miles from the City of Mexico, Gage often went to town for the day, no doubt following the road to the point where the stone aqueduct, which carried water to the capital from the springs at Chapultepec, turned into the outskirts of the city.

Beside the high arches of this aqueduct were neat and fertile squares of farmland, through which meandered a sluggish canal, thick with weed. There were seven of these canals crossing the city, their noisome waters flowing beneath pretty little bridges. Had they been kept clean, and had the water circulated more freely, no doubt these canals would have given the city a charm similar to that of Amsterdam. They were too narrow, though, for the density of the freight and passenger traffic which used them. Furthermore, they were, at certain times of the year, almost dry, and since there was no adequate system of garbage collection (although, Gage says, 'scavengers' were appointed), they received all the filth of the town. The Spaniards had not followed the example of the Aztecs, who, thrifty as Chinese peasants, had carried away the manure, night-soil and garbage of the city to be used as fertilizer.

Mexico City was quite large: there were between thirty and forty thousand Spaniards, eighty thousand Indians and *mestizos* (Gage much underestimates the size of this element of the population), and fifty thousand negroes and mulattoes, both slaves and freedmen. Thus, its white population alone was as great as that of the Bristol or Norwich Gage knew, and its total population of one hundred and sixty-five thousand (the Indians, mestizos, Negroes and mulattoes making up the lower, serf and slave classes) was nearly two-thirds that of London in 1603. It had a circumference of six miles. Yet, compared to the island-city, Tenochtitlan, it was a small town: exact population figures for Tenochtitlan are not available; but one reliable estimate gives the city itself a population of between five hundred and sixty thousand and seven hundred thousand, and what might be called Metropolitan Tenochtitlan, including the satellite villages, a population of over one million.

Nevertheless, it was, in many respects, a magnificent city. Beneath the hard gem-like blue of the plateau sky, there rose the towers, steeples and tiled domes of a colonial capital which had arisen in an age obsessed by the visual images of grandeur. There were fifty or more churches, convents, monasteries and hospitals; there were the ornate government buildings of stone and brick, and the low, wide-spreading houses of the rich, with their patios and flowers. There were the tidy shops of the city centre. But there were also the grim *obrajes*—workshops and factories—and, scattered in the suburbs, the wretched huts of those who had originally owned the land, and now supported it on their naked backs.

As to the houses of the wealthy, some were two storeys high, with French roofs, but most were in the Mediterranean style—low, extended and flat-roofed. Their walls rose beside the street; the eaves of wood or pottery would, in the rains of summer, pour torrents of water on to the road. They were built around courtyards and patios, invisible from the road, which contained pools, statues and flowering trees; and behind each house was a corral for horses and other domestic animals.

Their gates and doors opened directly on to the street, and many of them were deep-carved with coats of arms. Most of

61

the Creole aristocracy were *hidalgos*, or 'gentlemen', the lowest rank of the Spanish upper class. Some, it is true, were counts or marquises. As a rule, though, most Creole titles had been purchased; thus, while they may have been impressive enough in the New World, they were scorned in the Old.

'Their buildings are with stone and brick very strong, but not high, by reason of the many earthquakes, which would endanger their houses if they were above three storeys high. The streets are very broad, in the narrowest of them three coaches may go, and in the broader six may go in the breadth of them, which makes the city seem a great deal bigger than it is. In my time it was thought to be of between thirty and forty thousand inhabitant Spaniards, who are so proud and rich that half the city was judged to keep coaches, for it was a most credible report that in Mexico in my time there were above fifteen thousand coaches. It is a by-word that at Mexico four things are fair; that is to say, the women, the apparel, the horses, and the streets. But to this I may add the beauty of some of the coaches of the gentry, which do exceed in cost the best of the Court of Madrid and other parts of Christendom, for they spare no silver, nor gold, nor precious stones, nor cloth of gold, nor the best silks from China to enrich them. And to the gallantry of their horses the pride of some doth add the cost of bridles and shoes of silver.'

And clothing, Gage tells us, was equally extravagant—

'Both men and women are excessive in their apparel, using more silks than stuffs and cloth. Precious stones and pearls further much this their vain ostentation; a hat-band and rose made of diamonds in a gentleman's hat is common, and a hat-band of pearls is ordinary in a tradesman; nay, a blackamoor or tawny young maid and slave will make hard shift but she will be in fashion with her neck-chain and bracelets of pearls, and her ear-bobs of some considerable jewels. The attire of this baser sort of people of blackamoors and mulattoes (which are of a mixed nature, of Spaniards and blackamoors) is so light, and their carriage so enticing, that many Spaniards even of the better sort (who are too, too prone to venery) disdain their wives for them.'

Just before it reached the fashionable part of town, the aqueduct turned towards the convent of San Francisco. This was one of the great ecclesiastical complexes of the city: with its houses, gardens, hospital, monastery and church, it covered the equivalent of four modern city blocks. The viceroy attended church here, and here, in 1629, would be reinterred the bones of Hernan Cortés, the conqueror of Mexico. The church itself was built of stones from the great central pyramid of Tenochtitlan.

To the west of the Convent of San Francisco was a poor quarter, containing the College of San Juan de Letrán for mestizo boys, and another college for mestizo girls. Nearby, on marshy ground, were some wretched Indian hovels: they could not be seen from the main thoroughfare, since—to quote one Mexican writer's scornful exaggeration—they were built so low they scarcely seemed to lift themselves from the ground. They were scattered without order, the writer says, 'as is the ancient custom among them'. This area seems to have had something of the quality of a depressed Indian village, set on the outskirts of a large city. In this miserable quarter were a few shops, some of them owned by wealthy persons who, of course, lived elsewhere in the city, a public market, and a notably high gallows, built in a tower, and reached by a door and staircase.

Most of the Indians of the urban area had been forced into quarters like this one. Some of the descendants of the Aztec ruling class had become a semi-captive indigenous gentry, and were entitled to be called 'Don'. These lived with some dignity, their position being higher than that of their fellow mestizos and Indians, though below that of the Spanish gentry. The mestizos, as a rule, were in a lower middle class position: a mestizo would be considered successful if he had become a shop-keeper or a steward. The urban Indians, though, were being driven deeper and deeper into indigence. As Gage expresses it, 'The Spaniards daily cozen them of the small plot of ground where their houses stand, and of three or four houses of Indians build up one good and fair house after the Spanish fashion with gardens and orchards. And so is almost all Mexico new built with very fair and spacious houses with gardens of recreation.'

Indian education, conducted by the earliest missionaries on a high level of idealism, had deteriorated; and the time was fast approaching when persons of mixed blood would be barred from the universities, because it was claimed, there were too many of them appearing in the professions. It was difficult enough, if one was an Indian, to be a 'poor but honest' workman. In most of the guilds, which were poisonous with lower-class white prejudice, an Indian could not hope to advance beyond the status of a journeyman. Indeed, it was hard for him to be accepted as an apprentice. Usually he was hired as an unskilled labourer. The craftsmanship of the Indian was universally recognized by persons of taste, yet he had to work for very low pay, and without the protection of the guilds, who feared his competition.

San Francisco was only one of the churches whose great domes rose above the confusion of lesser domes and spires. In the city's marshy southern quarter, encircled by private homes, there was San Agustin. It had just been rebuilt for the third time, its two predecessors having, says Gage, 'quite sunk away'. In the northern quarter, in a large enclosed square, there stood the church of Santiago Tlaltelolco. Not too far away was Santo Domingo, which had been surrounded, seventy-five years earlier, by a number of tall old houses:

Manila in 1660, from a drawing by Johannes Vingboons

1. Cañas muy largas: y pruesas deq sehacen andamios Cosas 8c. 2. Bongas conq se hace el buyo d que vsa todo genero de gentes mascādolo como
tabaco. 3. Murcielago muy grande con cabeza como perro. 4. Cocos, deq se saca agua, vino, aceite, tuba, &

Rural scene in the Philippines

Guadeloupe, as seen by Samuel de Champlain in 1599

here had lived the pioneer élite of Mexico City, the first descendants of the conquistadores.

The social centre of the city was the Alameda; and Gage's description of it is particularly vivid—

'The gallants of this city shew themselves daily, some on horseback, and most in coaches, about four of the clock in the afternoon in a pleasant shady field called *la Alameda*, full of trees and walks, somewhat like unto our Moorfields, where do meet as constantly as the merchants upon our exchange about two thousand coaches, full of gallants, ladies and citizens, to see and to be seen, to court and to be courted, the gentlemen have their train of blackamoor slaves, some a dozen, some half a dozen, waiting on them, in brave and gallant liveries, heavy with gold and silver lace, with silk stockings on their black legs, and roses on their feet, and swords by their side; the ladies also carry their train by their coach's side of such jet-like damsels as before have been mentioned for their light apparel, who with their bravery and white mantles over them seem to be, as the Spaniard saith, *"mosca in leche"*, a fly in milk. But the train of the Viceroy, who often goeth to this place, is wonderful stately, which some say is as great as the train of his master the King of Spain.

'At this meeting are carried about many sorts of sweetmeats and papers of comfits to be sold, for to relish a cup of cool water, which is cried about in curious glasses, to cool the blood of those love-hot gallants. But many times these meetings sweetened with conserves and comfits have sour sauce at the end, for jealousy will not suffer a lady to be courted, no nor sometimes to be spoken to, but puts fury into the violent hand to draw a sword or dagger and to stab or murder whom he was jealous of, and when one sword is drawn thousands are presently drawn, some to right the party wounded or murdered; others to defend the party murdering; whose friends will not permit him to be apprehended, but will guard him with drawn swords until they have conveyed him to the sanctuary of some church, from whence the Viceroy his power is not able to take him for a legal trial.

'Many of these sudden skirmishes happened whilst I lived about Mexico . . .'

Perhaps because the Inquisition was not very active in 1625, Gage fails to mention a great stone platform in the western section of this beautiful and fashionable garden. This was the *Quemadero*: it was here that the Inquisition burned heretics. The last great *autos* had been held towards the end of the preceding century: the next would be held during the 1640's. In both cases, the main victims were Marranos, crypto-Jews, who professed Christianity, but secretly practised Judaism. In both cases, economic jealousies would seem to have been as strong among the Creoles as theological zeal: the Jews were, for all the restrictions against them, virtual masters of the commercial system of the Spanish colonies, and were particularly strong in Mexico.

As Gage walked past the Alameda towards the central square, the Plaza Mayor, he would have been entering the section of the fashionable shops. As a general rule, each craft and commodity had a section of its own. Gage tells of

'the beautiful street called *La Plateria* or Goldsmiths Street, where a man's eyes may behold in less than an hour many millions' worth of gold, silver, pearls and jewels. The street of St Austin [San Agustin] is rich and comely, where live all that trade in silks; but one of the longest and broadest is the street called Tacuba, where almost all the shops are of ironmongers, and of such as deal in brass and steel.'

And there were other sections occupied by the workers in feathers, as well as the chandlers, saddle-makers, pastry-cooks and furniture-dealers. Many of the best craftsmen, he notes, are Indians and Christian Chinese: yet, while they handled the most precious materials every day, they somehow never managed to turn them into wealth for themselves.

Mexico was a great trading city; and one of the most colourful descriptions of its traffic is found in Balbuena's *La Grandeza Mexicana*, that curious poem, born between two ages, which has the content of a Chamber of Commerce booster's pamphlet, but is written in the rich allusive style, clotted with sensuous detail and brilliant with glittering images, of the Spanish Baroque. Says Balbuena, rhythmically jingling the heavy gold coins in his sleeve—

> *Riches and opulence are here complete,*
> *Since you'll find treasure here in greater store*
> *Than the cold north can freeze, or the sun heat.*
>
> *Silver extracted from Peruvian ore,*
> *And Chilean gold pour in here every day.*
> *Ternate's cloves, cinnamon of Tidore,*
>
> *Garnets of Ormuz, ransom of Quinsay,*
> *Syrian spikenard, incense of Araby,*
> *Sicilian coral, fine cloth from Cambrai,*
>
> *Diamonds from India, Goan ivory,*
> *Rubies and Scitan emeralds here are seen;*
> *And from Siam comes its grey ebony,*
>
> *With Macao's best, and the best Philippine*
> *Products, and the very best from Spain,*
> *And from both Javas riches peregrine.*

—and the reason for all this wealth is stated elsewhere in the poem—

> *Lucca has not, nor Florence, nor Milan,*
> *Nor any town where bills are promptly paid,*
> *And it's thought good to be a businessman,*
>
> *More noble or more generous a trade,*
> *Merchants more skilled; nor are there anywhere*
> *More goods, more bargains, or more profits made.*

In the great square at the centre of the city there had once stood the palaces and council-chambers of Montezuma and his nobles, the massive temple-crowned pyramids of Huit-zilopochtli and Tlaloc, and the great rack where the Aztecs displayed the skulls of their defeated enemies. With its cell-like stone temples, sacred pools, platforms and friezes set in a rigidly geometrical plan, the square had seemed a strange combination of elements: it was at once an Indian ceremonial centre, carried to the highest degree of formal perfection, and something distinctly reminiscent of an ancient Mediterranean temple complex.

Now, however, the Plaza Mayor was the centre of Spanish imperial and civic rule in Mexico. The new square, if not as formally overwhelming as the old, had the heavy authority and sumptuousness of the Baroque. Balbuena, who saw Mexico City not only as a new Carthage, but as a new Rome, and even a new Athens, describes—

> *The portals covered with sculpture—here's largess*
> *Of subtle craft, and here's the richest treasure*
> *Of Corinthian taste and Corinthian tenderness.*

> *Flutings and triglyphs subtly vary pleasure,*
> *And, with reliefs of gold in a wide frieze,*
> *Give the whole work proportion and due measure.*

On the east side of the square, very nearly on the site of Montezuma's palace, was the palace of the Viceroy. It presented to the square the stern façade of a fortress, with its clock-tower and its four lesser towers, its regularly spaced loop-holes, its two great gates with their ponderous carved doors, and the Royal Prison ('which is strong of stone work', Gage says) at one end of the edifice. But there were, behind the palace walls, apartments and courtyards of great beauty.

On the northwest corner of the square was the Cathedral of

Mexico, still under construction; its walls had been raised, some domes had been completed, and some wooden roofs laid. On the south side of the square was the municipal palace, where the city council sat. A canal, all that remained of the canoe-basin of Tenochtitlan's great square, ran in front of it. Freight canoes still discharged their cargoes here. On the second storey, there was an open corridor, and at ground level a long arcade running the full length of the building, 'built all with arches on the one side where people may walk dry in time of rain'. Here were the public auctioneers, and petty traders of all kinds: 'there are shops of merchants furnished with all sorts of stuffs and silks, and before them sit women selling all manner of fruits and herbs'. Here the royal officials weighed the silver as it came into the mint (which was just off the other side of the square, beside the Viceroy's Palace), and subtracted from it the tax known as 'The King's Fifth'. Here also was the municipal jail, and the city butcher, who worked under contract to the city.

In its own square, off the Plaza Mayor, was the first European university in America, founded in 1551 by decree of Charles the Fifth. It was not the first college as such, since the Aztecs did have institutions of higher learning, where one could study such subjects as history, good manners, the interpretation of dreams, and astrology. The curriculum of the Royal and Pontifical University of Mexico also included a course in astrology; but one could be excommunicated for casting a horoscope in Mexico, and the art, science, pseudo-science or whatever it may be, was mainly used as an aid in the compilation of almanacs.

This, then, was 'The Imperial, Pontifical and Ever August Mexican Athens' (to quote from an entertainment given at the University in 1683) 'of which city', Gage says, 'a whole volume might be compiled, but that by other authors much hath been written, and I desire not to fill my history with trifles, but only with what is most remarkable in it.'

VIII—*This New World of America*

AT this point, Gage leaves the narrative of his travels to give a description of those parts of North America which Spain claimed as her own. Anticipating what was to be a major preoccupation of the United States, as they expanded from a confederacy on the Atlantic coast into a continental empire, he points out that the Spaniards have declared their intention to conquer all this territory, unless the English 'from Virginia and their other plantations' get there first. He describes the dependence of the Plains' Indians on the buffalo, erring only in what seems to be a belief that they had domesticated them. His report is obviously based on the *Relación* of Casteñeda, a member of the Coronado expedition, which reached Kansas in 1541–2.

> 'The chief riches of this country are their kine, which are to them as we say of our ale to drunkards, meat, drink and cloth and more too: for the hides yield them houses, or at least the coverings of them; their bones, bodkins; their hair, thread; their sinews, ropes; their horns, their maws and their bladders, vessels; their dung, fire; their calves' skins, buckets to draw and keep water; their blood, drink; and their flesh, meat.'

Gage was also one of the first proponents of that theory of Indian origins most popular today; it is supposed by some, he says, that the inhabitants of these northern parts first came over to this New World from Tartary, since 'the west side of America, if it be not continent with Tartary, is yet disjoined but by a small strait'.

70

How had he heard of the strait, whose existence, it is commonly thought, was not suspected until it was discovered by Vitus Bering in 1727?

We do know from the Englishman, Henry Hawks, who travelled in Mexico between 1568 and 1572, that in that period ships were sailing north from Western Mexican ports to discover a western entrance to 'the strait that lies between Newfoundland and Greenland', that is, the Strait of Anian, 'but it was not found'. Earlier, a pilot of the Philippine fleet, Juan de Fuca, who in 1592 discovered the strait which bears his name, had been on such a mission, which had failed.

Gage may also have read, in Hakluyt, an account of the voyage in which Francisco Gali, a pilot on the Macao-Acapulco route, had touched the American coast at a latitude of 37° 30'. Gali had concluded, from the set of the ocean currents, that there was a strait between Asia and America.

Gage's interest in the remote hinterlands was not merely an academic one, nor did it arise from mere curiosity: his references to North America are all part of his campaign to persuade his readers that Britain has a future in America, and could be, if she acted boldly, its sole master. As he says in his preface, addressed to Lord Fairfax, '. . . why should my countrymen the English be debarred from making use of that which God from all beginning no question did ordain for the benefit of mankind?'

His writing is most vivid, though, when he is describing what he has seen himself. There is Chapultepec, 'Grasshopper Hill', near Mexico City, where those viceroys who had died in New Spain were buried, and where those Aztec emperors who had preceded them had also been buried; here 'there is a sumptuous palace built with many fair gardens and devices of water, and ponds of fish, whither the Viceroy and the gentry of Mexico resort for their recreation'.

One of his most picturesque passages describes the convent of La Soledad, also called *el desierto de los leones*. It was built in 1606 for the Discalced Carmelites, as a place of privation, self-torture and prayer. There the monks were expected to live a life as ascetic as that of the Egyptian anchorites of the Thebaid, or for that matter, the Aztec hermit Yappan, who, seeking to please the gods with his austerities, set up his solitary abode on a rock, only to be tempted to lust by the love-goddess Xochiquetzal.

La Soledad was a stately cloister set on a hill, and surrounded by huge rocks, into which cells had been cut. These cells, ten in number, were extremely austere: they were decorated only with religious pictures and images and 'rare devices for mortification, as disciplines of wire, rods of iron, haircloths, and girdles with sharp wire points to girdle about their bare flesh'.

The surroundings were far from austere, though. The cells were set in gardens and orchards some two miles in compass. Springs of water bubbled delightfully among the rocks, and the smell of roses lay heavy in the air. The pain of the hermits was, certainly, aromatic. They only spent a week there, carrying with them a good supply of wines and sweetmeats, and 'as for fruits, the trees about do drop them into their mouths'. The gardens were much frequented by fashionable people, who usually brought along a supply of delicacies for the hermits. It seems there was no sign forbidding this. They also left more expensive gifts. There was a picture in the Church of La Soledad, called our Lady of Carmel, which was surrounded by heaps of 'diamonds, pearls, golden chains and crowns, and gowns of cloth of gold and silver'. 'Before this picture', Gage says, 'did hang in my time twenty lamps of silver, the worst of them being worth a hundred pounds.'

72

IX—*Gage Runs Away*

GAGE lived in the house at San Jacinto from October to February. As we have seen, he spent much of this time wandering about Mexico City, but he was also careful to inquire into the state of the Philippines, which was, after all, his real destination. During this time he met a friar who had just returned from those islands. The friar's description was not encouraging.

The superiors in the Philippines were cruel, he said, punishing the friars with harsh penances for the smallest and most trifling offences. Some, unable to bear such treatment, had hanged themselves; others, less passive, had been hanged for murdering their superiors.

Yet, though small offences were ruthlessly punished, greater offences seem to have been common. The friar described Manila as a most wicked place, where it was almost impossible to avoid falling into grievous sin. He would have lost his soul forever, had he not escaped by stealth, after many times begging his superior to permit him to return to Spain.

He refused to say more about himself, evading all questions aimed at finding out why he had come away. He would say only that most of the Philippine friars were devils in private, though in public they took pains to appear as gentle as angels and as simple as sheep. Most of them, he said, spent their time studying how to acquire or use the wives and wealth of those under their care. Some of them had been found, in the dim light of morning, dangling on ropes at the gates of their cloisters—murdered and hung up there by the

73

husbands or lovers of their paramours. In some cases, their women had been hung up beside them.

Not all the friars were like this, of course. There were, no doubt, a few saintly men, and there must have been many of sound morals. Yet a number of the friars were, certainly, worldly creatures, and some of them must have more resembled transported convicts than men of God.

The Philippine Church was very rich. Individual traders, who risked their fortunes on a shipment of cargo as one might on a throw of the dice (the eastward Pacific crossing was one of the lengthiest and most dangerous known at the time), were always failing. The Church, however, never failed, not so much because it was built on a rock, but because it acted as a mercantile bank, advancing loans at a rate of twenty to fifty per cent. Since it had huge capital reserves, it could absorb the losses resulting from the bankruptcy of some of its creditors—whose hope of gain lay, with the bones of seamen, at the bottom of the Pacific—and rake in excellent profits from its good debts. It could also take land as security: by now the church held most of the great estates of the islands, which of course yielded them further profit. In Mexico also, it should be said, the religious orders did most of the banking, and held much of the land.

Certainly, much of the money made by these priestly financiers was spent on charitable works. The *obras pias*, such as the *Hermandad de la Misericordia*, performed such necessary tasks as the provision of dowries for poor girls, the relief of the poor, the care of prisoners, the education of orphans, and the support of hospitals and foreign missions. The rapacity of the Philippine church could not be compared with that of the merchants. It is significant, however, that such comparisons must be made, that in its secular actions the Philippine church (the same could be said of the Mexican) offered an example, not of a superior morality, but of a mitigated immorality.

To Gage, who was disillusioned, the friar's tale was the last straw. So he tells us, at least, attributing to himself the best possible motives. However, some moral indignation may have been justified. He came from a family which for more than fifty years had risked everything—possessions, peace of mind, life itself—in the Roman Catholic cause. Had they done all this so that the hermits of La Soledad might wolf sugared fruits in their cells, and Philippine friars, living on usury, might seduce the wives of Manila citizens?

Gage and four of his friends, including Tomás de León, the Irish friar, agreed that they would try to find some way of returning to Spain or remaining in Mexico. The pact had to be kept secret. Had Calvo heard of their intention, he would have imprisoned them in the cloister until the fleet left for the Philippines. They did approach some Mexican friars, to ask what the chances were of their being able to take refuge in some Mexican cloister. The answer was disheartening. There was such a bitter rivalry between the Creole and Spanish friars, the Mexicans said, that they would never be admitted, since nearly all Mexican convents were held by the Creole party. They might find refuge in the province of Oaxaca, where half the friars were from Spain. Their prospects would be even better in Guatemala: there most of the friars were from Spain, and persecuted and slighted those of their brethren who had been born in the country.

It was for this reason that they decided to go to Guatemala—a bold decision, since it was nine hundred miles away, and they possessed neither horses nor money of their own.

At about this time, a certain friar named Peter Borrallo decided, quite on his own, to run away. His destination was

75

the same as theirs—Guatemala. Now Calvo revealed that ruthless efficiency which his appearance, so fat, slovenly and jovial, hardly suggested. He prevailed on the Viceroy to order that the public crier proclaim Borrallo's escape in the market place, and add that any who should harbour Borrallo and refuse to deliver him up, or to hand over any other escaped Philippine friar, should be put in prison, and fined five hundred ducats.

Tomás de León, frightened, withdrew from the pact; and Gage, fearing that he might, in order to worm his way back into Calvo's favour, reveal their plans, pretended to be in agreement with him. The other three friars—Francisco de la Vega, Juan Escudero, and that same Antonio Meléndez who had persuaded Gage to leave Spain in the first place—were completely uncertain as to what they should do next.

At this point, de León drops out of the narrative. We know from other sources that he went to the Philippines with the Dominican mission. Dominican records show that he was sent to Cavite, after having served two years in Manila. There is no further record of him.

When de León was not within earshot, however, Gage continued to encourage his companions. You see, he said, what Calvo thinks of his friars, to have their escape cried aloud in the market-place, as if they were runaway slaves. Why should they consent to be shipped like cattle to the other end of the world? In any case, he had heard privately that Borrallo had been seen, far from Mexico City, travelling alone towards Guatemala. Could they not escape as well as he?

It was agreed, therefore, that the night before the mission left for Acapulco to join the Manila fleet, the four would slip away from San Jacinto. Two by two, they would go to Mexico City, where they would have horses waiting. They would travel by night, until they had gone some twenty or thirty leagues. Calvo would not delay to search for them, since, if he and his company missed the sailing of the fleet, he would have to wait another year in Mexico. It is true that the Viceroy had appointed officers to watch the chief roads out of the city until the Dominican mission left for Acapulco, but they could easily avoid capture by leaving Mexico City through the side streets.

A 'friend', whom Gage does not name, had offered to guide them out of the city by an obscure route: he had also prepared a map for them. It was decided they would leave through the suburb of Guadelupe, thus giving the impression that they were heading away from Guatemala, rather than towards it.

After the four had purchased their horses, they pooled their money in a common purse. They found they had only twenty ducats, or slightly more than twenty English shillings in purchasing power. Yet they resolved to go on, relying, as Gage tells us, more on the Providence of God than on any earthly means.

They left around the middle of February—just in time— at ten in the evening, and they travelled comfortably till dawn. At a little Indian town, they ordered a turkey and a capon, and breakfasted with their mysterious friend and guide before he returned to Mexico. They slept for the rest of that day, and set out again at nightfall. When they reached the town of Atlixco, they stayed at a farm, set well back from the main highway.

They were already beginning to feel more at ease. They were not, after all, sleeping in barns, and nobody seemed to regard them with suspicion. The richer farmers and yeomen they encountered were honoured by their visit, and entertained them sumptuously; they had great respect for priests and friars, and nobody was presumptuous enough to ask them where they had come from, and where they were going. Usually, when they left, their hosts gave them money. By the time they were forty leagues out of Mexico, the common purse had doubled its weight; they had forty ducats.

In the valley of San Pablo, not far from Atlixco, they came upon a farm owned by a countryman of Meléndez', who had come from the friar's own town of Segovia, in Spain. For the sake of Segovia, this yeoman kept them with him three days and nights. He was well off: his sideboard was full of silver bowls and cups; his table was set with plates rather than wooden trenchers, and his daughters were trained in music. The valleys around Mexico were full of such farmers, who, like their North American counterparts of more than a century later, had vastly improved their condition in the New World.

From San Pablo—they were following, deliberately, a very circuitous route—they came to Taxco, then a small hill-built town of some five hundred inhabitants. Then, after moving through some smaller towns, they came to Oaxaca— a small city of about two thousand inhabitants, Gage tells us, yet fair and pleasant to the eye. It was the centre of a rich cattle and sheep district; the religious houses were notably well off, and the town was particularly well-known for its chocolate, which was put up in boxes by the nuns of one of the convents, and sent all over Mexico, and, indeed, as far as Spain.

Here they were informed of a law most convenient to religious travellers. The Indians were obliged to provide, free of charge, to all friars passing through their towns, a change of horses and food to carry them farther on their journey, provided only that the friars stayed no longer than twenty-four hours. At their departure, the cost of this service was to be entered in the town book, which at the end of the year was to be shown to the Spanish justice under whose jurisdiction they were. The amount would then be repaid from the proceeds of the sale of the wheat or maize grown on the common plot of the town.

Here, also, they encountered for the first time unmistakable evidence of the virulence of the hatred which existed between the native-born Spanish-Mexicans and the *gachupines* from Spain.

There had been in Oaxaca a grave old friar from Spain. He was a Master of Divinity, and noted through the entire valley for his learning. Yet, because he was from Spain, his reputation had only aroused the hatred and envy of the Mexican friars. While he was alive, they had been unable to discover anything against him. But after he had died, they had discovered in his chamber a coffer containing a sum of money which he had not, while he was alive, declared to his superior. The old man violated his vows, they cried; he has died in sin. So they buried the learned old man, and his reputation with him, in the middle of the garden of the convent. The entire valley cried out against the friars for this act; yet they responded by saying that since he had committed a sin worthy of excommunication, and had neither confessed it nor made restitution, he had died excommunicate.

Yet all of them, Gage tells us, were guilty of this same sin of making their vocations pay; some of those who condemned the old man must have sinned much more greatly than he. It was because he was from Spain that they did this, he says, so great a hatred did they bear to the *gachupines*, who both by law and custom occupied all the high positions in the country.

The four renegade friars decided they would not stay in

Oaxaca. What security would they have, three Spaniards and a Hispanified Englishman, in this snake-pit of intrigue? They might at any moment be condemned and turned over to the secular authorities, to be shipped, under heavy censure, to Manila.

After three days, they decided to move on. Their destination was Chiapa, which was three hundred miles from Oaxaca, and part of the Dominican province of Guatemala. They thus began to travel towards Tehuantepec, which was on the shore of the Pacific, and stood at the beginning of the Guatemala road.

X—From Tehuantepec to Chiapa

TEHUANTEPEC was a fishing town: you could meet on the roads long trains of fifty to a hundred mules, their backs piled high with salt fish for Oaxaca, Puebla and Mexico. It was also a small and prosperous port whose merchants, some of whom were very rich, traded with Peru and other colonies to the south.

When Gage and his companions arrived in Tehuantepec, they found they had the choice of two roads: they could take the coast road to Guatemala, which passed through the provinces of Soconusco and Suchitepequéz, or the mountain road which would take them to Chiapa, through wild and rocky country. They chose the latter.

As they rode away from Tehuantepec, the land became drier. After they had passed through the little town of Ixtepec, they found themselves in a desert—the beach sand to their right, and to their left an earth almost as dry as sand. The water courses were only dry cracks in the earth; the

Vera Cruz and San Juan de Ulloa, as seen by Champlain in 1599

Mexico City in 1628—the celebrated *Vista* of Juan Gomez de Trasmonte green of the scanty vegetation—low brush, organ cactus, and one or two trees deserving of the name—was dull with dust.

They travelled through the desert for two days. There were no towns or houses; there were only, at wide-spaced intervals, thatched lodges for the shelter of travellers. One night they did not reach a lodge before nightfall, and slept on the ground. The plain was open to the sea: the wind blew continually, and with such strength that they were almost blown off their horses. Occasionally they would see a few cattle or some wild horses, but they encountered no human beings.

On the second day, Gage became separated from his three companions. They had ridden on ahead, hastening to reach the next town before night-fall. Gage, who was having trouble with his horse, was following them at some distance. The horse grew more and more obstinate: finally it refused to move any farther. Gage dismounted, intending to lead the animal to the town, which he knew could not be far; but at this point, the horse lay down.

Gage now had two alternatives, neither of them attractive. He could stay where he was. He could set out for the town on foot, leaving his horse to browse; but in that great flat plain, with not a hedge, tree or shrub to mark the place or hide the saddle, he might never find him again.

He decided therefore to pass the night where he was, hoping his friends would send from the town to see what had become of him. He unsaddled his horse, and lay down to rest, using the saddle as a pillow.

He lay there for about an hour, watching his horse feeding on the short, withered grass. He was about to go to sleep, when he heard a fearful howling, barking and crying. At first, when it was a good distance away, it sounded to him like the noise made by a pack of dogs. When it came closer, he realized that it was not a sound such as dogs make; there seemed to be human shrieks intermingled with the animal noises. Now it was an age still acutely aware of the supernatural, and Gage, so many times a renegade, had an uneasy conscience—

'Sometimes I thought of witches, sometimes of devils, sometimes of Indians turned into the shape of beasts (which amongst some hath been used), sometimes of wild and savage beasts, and from all these thoughts I promised myself nothing but sure death, for the which I prepared myself, recommending my soul to the Lord, whilst I expected my body should be a prey to cruel and merciless beasts; or some instruments of that roaring lion who in the Apostle goeth about seeking whom he may devour. I thought I could not anyways prevail by flying or running away, but rather might that way run myself into the jaws of death; to hide there was no place, to lie still I thought was safest, for if they were wild beasts, they might follow their course another way from me, and so I might escape. Which truly proved my safest course, for while I lay sweating and panting, judging every cry, every howling and shrieking an alarm to my death, being in this agony and fearful conflict till about midnight, on a sudden the noise ceased, sleep (though but the shadow of death) seized upon my wearied body, and forsook me not, till the morning's glorious lamp, shining before my slumbering eyes and driving away death's shadow, greeted me with life and safety.'

Blinking, and looking about him, Gage saw that his horse was still there. He expressed in prayer his gratitude for having lived through the terrors of the night; then he rose from his knees, and saddled his horse. He wanted nothing so keenly as to be out of that place.

After he had ridden rather more than a mile, he came upon a brook, where two roads met. One led through the desert; he could gaze down that road for five or six miles, and see neither a house nor a tree. The other led to a small grove of trees, some two or three miles off. Here, he thought, there might be a town.

After he had ridden a quarter of a mile farther, his horse grew stubborn again. Gage dismounted, and led his mount by the bridle, until, as he approached a thatched house by the side of the road, he saw an Indian riding towards him. Gage asked him the distance to the nearest town. The Indian answered that it was just beyond the trees, but Gage would not see it until he was almost on top of it. Encouraged now, Gage mounted again, and spurred and prodded his horse until they came to the trees. There the horse stopped, and refused to go any farther. Gage tethered him, unsaddled him, hid the saddle under some low shrubs, and entered the town on foot. Soon he found his friends. Not in the least suspecting that he had spent the night in the desert, they had sent to another town to inquire if he had been seen there.

When Gage told the Indians of the fearful noise which had kept him awake and in terror, they answered that they heard such howlings every night: they were only the cries of 'wolves and tigers', which came to steal their livestock. They commonly frightened them away with sticks or holloaings.

The next morning, after Gage had sold his horse and hired another, the four set out again.

They moved from town to town, encountering no difficulty and braving no danger or deprivation. They were usually entertained by the Indians or by the local priest, and they seem to have been entertained well. Eventually they came to Tapanatepec, at which point the land began to rise into the Chiapa Highlands. These were frightening mountains, and they had heard terrible stories of them. It was said they were the most dangerous mountains in Mexico, and that, near the peaks, one had to pass through some very high narrow passes, through which the winds from the Pacific, whose wrinkled skin one could see far below, rushed with such fury that they had on occasion blown laden mules, and horses with their riders, to a bloody death. Nevertheless, the friars decided they would face the passes, provided only the winds were not too boisterous on the day they began the climb.

Tapanatepec, nestling at the foot of this range, was an attractive and prosperous village. The climate was spring-like. The wealthier Indians had from a thousand to four thousand cattle on their estates; the sea, and the little river which ran by the town, were rich in fish; and the many streams, falling from the mountains which overshadowed the town, watered fertile market-gardens and orchards of orange, lemon and fig.

They set off up the mountain of Macuilapa in the afternoon. They were on muleback. Two Indians were guiding them, and in their saddlebags were fruit, fried fish and a cold roasted capon. They had been told that they need only climb some twenty-one English miles through the dangerous part of the mountains. After that, it was said, they would reach a country of wealthy ranchers, chief among whom was one Don Juan de Toledo, who would make them welcome. That night, they camped in a green meadow tucked away between two of Macuilapa's rocky ribs. They ate their capon and most of their fish, leaving only a few scraps for breakfast; then they turned in, lulled to sleep by the trickling of the brooks down the side of the mountain.

In the morning, they continued the climb. They had gone barely a mile when the wind began to whistle about them, and they were afraid. They thought of returning, though they were only halfway up the mountain; but the guides encouraged them, saying that there was a spring about a mile farther on, and that there they would find a lodge, built under the trees to shelter travellers.

They took refuge in the lodge that night, the more grateful for the trees around it, which broke the incessant pressure of the wind. They began to wish they had kept some of the provisions they had so thoughtlessly eaten, even some of the refuse they had thrown away: they would gladly have sucked the head of a fried fish, if they had thought to save one. At last, while they were searching among the trees around the lodge, they found a lemon tree. It had gone wild, and its fruit was small, green and very sour. Nevertheless, they plucked it greedily, and the flesh of green lemons, its acidity somewhat diluted by water from the spring, was their supper that night.

The next morning, they had more green lemons for breakfast. In the early afternoon, one of the friars, his eye sharpened by hunger, noticed that the Indians carried with them, as travel rations, little bags of powdered maize. They bought half a bag, for which the Indians charged them the equivalent of two shillings. In Tapanatepec, it might have been worth a penny.

Over Tuesday and Wednesday they waited for the wind to die down, living, for those two days, on green lemons, maize powder and water. On Thursday morning, the wind was as strong as ever; but they resolved to try the pass, since they were weakening, and might well starve to death, or die of sickness, on the side of Macuilapa.

Upon the bark of a giant tree they wrote their names, and the number of days they had been in the lodge without food. Then, feebly mounting their mules, they began to climb once again.

The way grew narrow and steep, and they alighted from their mules, thinking themselves safer on their own feet. Every hour, as they climbed, the wind grew stronger.

When they reached the top of the Macuilapa pass, they found it to be a bare rocky place with not a tree, not even a shrub to hinder the fury of the wind. They were on a ridge which was, in places, no more than forty-five inches wide. On one side they could see, horribly far below, the dazzling expanse of the Pacific; on the other side, they could see a rocky descent of, Gage says, six or seven miles. They crept forward on this narrow ridge of rock: the Indians led the way, and the friars, weakened by hunger, not daring to look to either side but staring at the ground, followed them on all fours. Their habits whipping in the wind, they inched forward, placing their hands and knees in the prints left by the hooves of the mules.

After what seemed hours of this frightful progress, the track widened, and they approached a clump of trees. They lay down, gasping with exhaustion, cursing themselves for their folly in seeking to travel the direct route over Macuilapa.

In any case, they were out of danger now, and so relieved were they that they moved, in spite of their weakness, with fair speed. Soon they arrived at the ranch of Don Juan de Toledo, who gave them some warm broth; but they were so weak that they promptly vomited it up again. After taking many small sips of broth and wine, they found they had recovered enough strength by nightfall to be able to cope with supper.

They rested two days with Don Juan de Toledo, and on the third they set out for Chiapa de Corzo.

XI—*Chiapa*

CHIAPA DE CORZO was, in Gage's time, called Chiapa of the Indians, to distinguish it from Chiapa proper, which was inhabited by Spaniards. It overlooked the Grivalja, which river, Gage states, is as broad as the Thames at London. It was a prosperous town: its Indian governor, Don Felipe de Guzmán, kept a dozen horses in his stable, was allowed to wear a rapier and dagger, and had not only sued the governor of Spanish Chiapa over some privileges of the town, but had actually won his case. 'No town', says Gage, 'hath so many dons in it of Indian blood as this.'

Here Gage and his companions were well-received by their fellow Dominicans. The Provincial and Chief Superior, they were told, would be glad to see them: the Creole and native friars, striving to control the convent as their countrymen controlled those in Mexico City, had the few Spaniards at a disadvantage. There was no doubt the newcomers would be taken in.

Here, by what would at first seem to be an amazing coincidence, they met Peter Borrallo, whose earlier escape had encouraged them in their own. In fact, though, there was nothing amazing about their meeting: there were not that many roads from Mexico into Guatemala, and Borrallo, as a Dominican, would be staying, as he travelled, in Dominican houses. Borrallo told them they had nothing to fear: he had been treated very kindly, and, in any case, Calvo and his train had already sailed from Acapulco. True, Calvo had loosed a Parthian shot on his departure: he had written a harsh letter to the Superior of Chiapa and Guatemala, in which he had asked him to order his provincials not to shelter Borrallo, Gage and their friends, but to send them back to Mexico under guard, so that they might be held there till the sailing of the next fleet for the Philippines. However, the Provincial in Chiapa, Father Pedro Álvarez, had not paid the slightest attention to the letter, and Borrallo had not been molested.

Álvarez was now in a little town just a day's journey from

Chiapa de Corzo. They decided to present themselves to him there. Since they could not hope to find refuge in any other part of America, they would ask him if they could either stay in Chiapa and Guatemala, or return to Spain.

When they arrived, they found him walking through one of the shady byways of the town. He entertained them that night, speaking to them in a gentle and fatherly manner; and before they went to bed, he washed their feet with his own hands.

That first day, he said almost nothing on the subject of their continuing under his jurisdiction. The next day, though, he produced the letter from Calvo, and read it aloud, adding his own severe comments—that they had sinned in forsaking their call to the Philippines, that they might have saved many Filipinos who would now be damned for having been denied missionaries of their ability, that they had betrayed and disappointed their King, at whose expense they had travelled from Spain, and, finally, that they must consider themselves his prisoners, and that he was empowered to ship them back to continue their journey, as Calvo had demanded. In the meantime, since he did not know what to do with them, they should take their ease in the grounds of the house he was now staying in. After dinner he would have an answer to a letter he had written to the Superior in Chiapa.

He then showed them into the garden.

They paced back and forth in the shade of the orange trees. Their spirits were low. Álvarez had talked in high terms: he had used words like 'souls', 'king', and 'imprisonment'. Could they doubt that they would be shipped back to Mexico? Each friar dwelt on his own black thoughts: Gage thought to himself that he would never see England again, but would moulder his life away in the Far East; Meléndez wished he were anywhere but where he was, even on the high pass at Macuilapa; another wished he had never flown from Mexico, but had gone quietly to the Philippines with Calvo. What could they do? One proposed that they try to escape from Álvarez, but another answered that no matter where they fled in Guatemala, they would be discovered. Even if they were sent to Mexico, he said, it would be easier to escape from the party escorting them there than from their present semi-captivity. Gage himself added some cogent arguments—that the Provincial had received them gently, even washing their feet as Our Lord had washed the feet of His apostles, that he could hardly condemn them for having come all that way to seek his protection and to offer themselves 'as fellow-labourers in that harvest of souls belonging to his charge', that he wanted Spaniards to counter-balance the Creole faction, that since he had accepted Borrallo he would hardly reject them, and, finally, that even if he did not accept them there, he would probably send them to Spain rather than to Mexico.

While they were thus exchanging worries and doubtful solutions, old Álvarez was watching them from his window. He sent another friar out to them, who asked them, as he approached, why they were so melancholy. The Provincial, said the friar, had observed their sadness. They should know that their melancholy was unjustified. The Provincial wished them well, and needed them; and since they had thrust themselves on his mercy, he would hardly be so cruel as to do to them what martial law forbade even a soldier to do to his defeated enemy.

The Creole faction, he added, had harshly censured the Provincial for sheltering Peter Borrallo: there could be no doubt that they would complain even more bitterly at the arrival of four more *gachupines*, and renegades at that. The Provincial could hardly be blamed for wanting to consider

the matter well. For their parts, they should carry themselves with such discretion that those who condemned even
the best of the Provincial's actions would have no arguments
against their staying. In any case, if for some reason they
could not be admitted into Chiapa or Guatemala, they
would not be sent back to Mexico, but would be allowed to
return to Spain.

Now the bell rang for dinner; and Gage, who could
always be cheered by the prospect of a good meal, went in
with a light heart, followed by his three renegade companions
and the Chiapan friar.

After dinner, the Provincial invited them to a game of
backgammon. Gage, in spite of his strictures against clerical
gambling, gladly assented. In any case, they were not to play
for money. Since I know you are poor, the Provincial said,
we will play on the following terms: if I win you owe me
five *Pater Nosters* and five *Ave Marias*, but if I lose I will be
compelled to admit you into the province.

The game began. The three young friars, taking turns one
after the other, were too much, as it seemed, for the old man;
but Gage, who was more acute, sensed that he was willing to
lose 'that his very losses might speak unto us what through
policy and discretion he would not utter with words'. Indeed,
a messenger arrived as soon as they had finished the game,
bearing a letter from the Prior in Chiapa. The Prior, replying
to the Provincial, expressed great joy at the arrival of the
four friars, and begged that they be sent him immediately,
to be his guests. For, he said, their case had been his some
two years before. He too had been in a company of Philippine missionaries; he too had deserted them, and fled to
Guatemala. He was glad to welcome them; and, he added
significantly, he hoped they would join with him against
those who spited him—that is, the Creoles.

Álvarez declared himself to be very pleased by this letter; as to the game of backgammon, he would now pay them what he had lost. The next day, he said, he would send them to Chiapa. They must stay there until he was ready to send them to other parts of the province, where they would learn the languages of the Indians, and preach to them.

The four friars went into the garden once again, but this time they were in a happier frame of mind. Indeed, they began to play there like children, laughing, joking and pelting each other with oranges and lemons, their particular target being the friar (probably the sub-deacon Juan Escudero) who had wished he were on the boat with Calvo. 'We strived to beat him out of the garden by force of orange and lemon bullets; which sport we continued the more willingly, because we perceived the good Provincial stood behind a lattice in a balcony beholding us, and rejoicing to see our hearts so light and merry.'

After supper, they had another game of backgammon with the Provincial; and now the stakes were different: if they won, he would give them a box of chocolate, and if they lost they would be his prisoners. This time the Provincial won: in fact he was such a cunning player that he could win any game he chose. I am sorry you have lost, he said, but I hope that you will never be prisoners to a worse enemy than I am. To console them, he would give each of them a box of chocolate, and they must drink some of that chocolate, for his sake and for their own comfort, when they were most disheartened by their imprisonment. They thought this was nothing more than a kindly joke, and they paid little attention to it.

In the morning, there were mules waiting for them, and an escort of twelve mounted Indians. They said goodbye to the Provincial, and set out for the town of San Felipe.

On their arrival, they met the Prior of Chiapa, Father Juan Batista. He took them to breakfast, with the rather disquieting remark that they would do well to eat heartily, since their dinner that night would be the meanest thing they had ever eaten. He further admonished them to enjoy their liberty, since it would not last long. They had been told they were out of danger, so they did not know how to take the remark. Was it a threat, or a mock-sadistic joke? After breakfast, the Indians of San Felipe entertained them with horse-races and *juego de cañas*, a sort of jousting. But they could not stay long, since they were expected to arrive in the cloister of Chiapa, two miles away, before noon. Their mules were brought to them; and the Indian singers and trumpeters (as a conquered and now servile race, the Indians were expected to do this kind of thing) escorted them 'with dances, music and ringing of bells' a half-mile out of town. Then the Prior dismissed them.

When they were within half a mile of Chiapa, the Prior ordered them to halt. He took a paper from his pocket, an order from the Provincial; and he proceeded to read it aloud in a formal manner. It said:

'. . . That whereas we had forsaken our lawful Superior Calvo in the way to the Philippines, and without his licence had come unto the province of Chiapa, he could not in conscience but inflict some punishment upon us before he did enable us to abide there as members under him; therefore he did strictly command the Prior of Chiapa that as soon as we should enter into his cloister, he would shut us up by two and two in our chambers, as in prisons, for three days, not suffering us to go out to any place, save only to the public place of refection (called refectory) where all the friars met together to dine and sup, where at noon time we were to present ourselves before all the cloisters sitting upon the bare ground, and there to receive no other dinner but only bread and water; but at supper we might have in our chambers, or prisons, what the Prior would be pleased to allow us.'

The Prior, noting their sadness, added a comforting postscript of his own. He assured them that after their short imprisonment, they would be honoured and preferred, and that, though their dinners should be of bread and water, he would afterwards send them a good supper to their chambers, which would more than sustain them for the next twenty-four hours. Thus encouraged, they proceeded to the cloister of Chiapa, where most of the friars greeted them cordially. But the faces of some, they noticed, were surly and frowning.

Almost as soon as they had been conducted to their chambers, the dinner-bell rang. It summoned them, however, to something less than a dinner. They went down to the refectory, and after grace had been said and the friars of the convent had seated themselves, the four 'Philippine Jonahs' (as some of the Creoles had decided to call them) sat crosslegged, 'like tailors', on the bare ground. Each of them received a loaf of bread and a pot of water.

A Creole friar was sitting beside them, doing penance for having written some love-letters to a nun. He did not consider his sin as great as theirs, and, perhaps to disguise his own sense of shame, he looked at them with an expression of exaggerated disgust. Gage (one of his redeeming features appears to have been a certain mischievous quality) chose a place as near to him as possible. The friar, under his breath, muttered 'disobedient Philippine Jonahs', to which Gage responded, in a soft and friendly tone, with two hexameters, invented on the spot—

Si monialis amor te turpia scribere fecit,
Ecce tibi frigidae praebent medicamina lymphae.

93

(If love for a nun made thee write scandalous things,
Lo, cold waters furnish thee their medicines.)

The friar, much offended, tried to remove himself (his penance forbade him to rise until dinner was over) by wriggling his elbows and shoulders and inching away on his buttocks; but Gage followed him in the same manner, adding—

Solamen misero est socios retinere pañetes.

(It is a solace to one in trouble to recall that a trouser leg always keeps its partner.)

The friar thought Gage was after the loaf which he was busily gnawing, so he hugged it closer to his breast. But the word *pañetes*—a Spanish word for a kind of trousers—so amused him in its Latin context that he began to laugh, and almost choked on his mouthful of bread.

Having eaten their meagre dinners, the four Jonahs returned to their cells. Shortly after, the Spanish friars began to crowd in, bringing them conserves, sweetmeats and other dainties, and begging them to tell their story. The Prior himself supped with them that night, and the food was excellent.

Even their being deprived of liberty over the next three days was a favour rather than a punishment, since it enabled them to rest after their long journey.

When they were set at liberty, the Provincial and Prior began to consider what might be done with them. Eventually two of the friars (Gage does not give their names) were sent into the country to learn the local Indian language. Gage and the remaining friar asked to be sent to the famous university at Guatemala, to study philosophy and divinity. This was agreed to, but it was decided that nothing could be done until Michaelmas, the beginning of the 'school year'.

In the meantime, the Provincial had heard of Gage's

94

extempore Latin verses. A teacher of grammar and syntax was needed in the school attached to the Chiapa cloister, and since English scholars were thought at that time to be better Latinists than the Spaniards, he appointed Gage to this position, granting him an allowance for books and other necessaries.

Gage remained in this position from April to the end of September.

Chiapa, a poor town of no more than four hundred Spanish householders, was served by a cathedral, and by two cloisters —one of Dominicans, the other of Franciscans. In additions there were about a hundred Indian families in a suburb, with a chapel of their own. The fact that there were no Jesuits in Chiapa, says Gage, is a proof of the poverty of most of the inhabitants, and the miserliness of the few rich ones, Jesuits usually attach themselves, 'like horse-leeches', to the wealthy and gallant. In Chiapa, however, the merchant: hugged their wealth to their bosoms, and the gentlemen were a wretched, threadbare, penurious lot.

'The gentlemen of Chiapa are a by-word all about that country, signifying great dons (*dones*, gifts or abilities, I should say), great birth, fantastic pride, joined with simplicity, ignorance, misery and penury. These gentlemen will say they descend from some duke's house in Spain, and immediately from the first Conquerors; yet in carriage they are but clowns, in wit, abilities, parts and discourse as shallow-brained as a low brook, whose waters are scarce able to leap over a pebble stone, any small reason soon tries and tires their weak brain, which is easily at a stand when sense is propounded, and slides on speedily when nonsense carrieth the stream . . . As presumptuous they are and arrogant as if the noblest blood in the Court of Madrid ran through their veins. It is a common thing amongst them to make a dinner only with a dish of *frijoles* in black broth, boiled with pepper and garlic, saying it is the most nourishing meat in all the Indies; and after this so stately a dinner they will be sure to come out to the street-door of their houses to see and be seen, and there for half an hour will they stand shaking off the crumbs of bread from their clothes, bands (but especially from their ruffs when they used them), and from their mustachios. And with their tooth-pickers they will stand picking their teeth, as if some small partridge bone stuck in them; nay, if a friend pass by at that time, they will be sure to find out some crumb or other in the mustachio (as if on purpose the crumbs of the table had been shaken upon their beards, that the loss of them might be a gaining of credit for great housekeeping) and they will be sure to vent out some non-truth, as to say: *O Señor, que linda perdiz he comida hoy*, "O Sir, what a dainty partridge have I eat today", whereas they pick out nothing from their teeth but the black husk of a dry *frijol* or Turkey bean.'

As for the women, they were equally bizarre creatures. So weak and squeamish were their stomachs, they claimed, that they must always be drinking chocolate, even in church. Indeed, during a solemn high Mass, the cathedral was more like a coffee-house than a church: there were always a number of maids bustling about, bringing their mistresses chocolate or taking away the empty cups.

Just before Gage had come, the Bishop had forbidden the drinking of chocolate in the cathedral, and when this had had no effect, he had fixed a notice to the church door, to the effect that all who drank chocolate or nibbled sweetmeats during Mass would be excommunicated. From this moment, the women of the town conceived a great hatred for the Bishop. Some of them missed no opportunity to insult or slight him; others simply continued to drink chocolate in church as they had before. One day, when the canons and other priests attempted to take away the cups of chocolate

96

from the maidservants, the women's husbands drew their swords against them, and they had to retire to avoid bloodshed.

Finally it became clear to the ladies that the Bishop would neither be persuaded nor coerced, and they decided to leave the Cathedral. Most of the fashionable people of the city resorted to the cloister churches. There was a degree of rivalry between the secular priests and the religious orders; and the result was that the cloisters grew rich, and the Cathedral, deprived of its offerings, grew poor.

At this, the Bishop posted another order, demanding that everybody in the city resort to the Cathedral. The response of the women was to stay at home. For a month the ladies of Chiapa did not attend church at all.

Now the Bishop developed an inexplicable sickness. Eventually he went to the Dominican cloister, where his friend, the Prior, took care of him. The doctors came; and it was their unanimous opinion that the Bishop had been poisoned. None of them could save him, and he weakened from day to day. He died, praying that those who had caused his death might be forgiven, and that the sacrifice of his life, offered for the honour of God and in the zeal of His house, would prove acceptable in His sight.

The common talk around town was that the Bishop had been poisoned by a gentlewoman who was somewhat too familiar with one of the Bishop's pages. It was said that she had, through this page, sent him a cup of poisoned chocolate. To the ladies, this seemed no more than poetic justice. Gage himself heard this gentlewoman say that few grieved for the Bishop, least of all the ladies, and that she supposed, since he was such an enemy of chocolate in church, that the chocolate he had drunk at home had not agreed with him either.

Afterwards it became a proverb in that country: 'Beware of the chocolate of Chiapa.'

The story is not so fantastic as it appears. The air of Chiapa was poisonous with rivalry and conflict. The Creoles resented the economic power of the church, even while they supported it; but they resented even more those few priests, zealous for justice, who condemned them for their greed, materialism, and ruthless exploitation of the Indians.

Fray Bartolomé de las Casas, that zealous if unbalanced fighter against oppression, had been Bishop of Ciudad Real de Chiapa in the preceding century. He had found the experience discouraging. In his time (the middle 1500's), he could remember only two governors and one bishop who had 'feared God, or obeyed God's laws or the King's': the colonists, for their part, replied that Las Casas was an 'ill-humoured, unquiet, importunate, noisy, trouble-making fellow', a complaint which has been made against other socially-conscious priests, in other places.

Perhaps the key to this story is to be found in Gage's statement that the Bishop was, though somewhat covetous, 'very zealous to reform whatever abuses [were] committed in the church'. Moral zeal was a rather dangerous virtue in seventeenth-century Mexico; it was particularly dangerous in Chiapa.

In fact Gage himself, by rejecting the advances of the suspected poisoner, placed himself in some danger.

'The women of this city are somewhat light in their carriage, and have learned from the Devil many enticing lessons and baits to draw poor souls to sin and damnation; and if they cannot have their wills, they will surely work revenge either by chocolate or conserves, or some fair present, which shall surely carry death along with it. The gentlewoman that was suspected (nay was questioned for the death of the Bishop) had often used to send me boxes of chocolate or conserves, which I willingly received from her, judging it to be a kind of gratuity for the pains I took in teaching her son Latin. She was of a very merry and pleasant disposition, which I thought might consist without sin, until one day she sent unto me a very fair plantain wrapped up in a handkerchief, buried in sweet jasmins and roses; when I untied the handkerchief, I thought among the flowers I should find some rich token, or some pieces of eight, but finding nothing but a plantain, I wondered, and looking further upon it, I found worked upon it with a knife the fashion of a heart with two of blind Cupid's arrows sticking in it, discovering unto my heart the poisoned heart and thoughts of the poisoner that sent it. I thought it a good warning to be wary and cautious of receiving more presents and chocolate from such hands, and so returned unto her again her plantain with this short rhyme cut out with a knife upon the skin, *Fruta tan fria, amor no cria*, as much as to say, fruit so cold, takes no hold. This answer and resolution of mine was soon spread over that little city, which made my gentlewoman outrageous, which presently she showed by taking away her son from school, and in many meetings threatening to play me a Chiapaneca trick. But I remembered the Bishop's chocolate and so was wary, and stayed not long after in that poisoning and wicked city, which truly deserves no better relation than what I have given of the simple dons, and the chocolate-confectioning donnas.'

XII—*Chimaltenango*

By the end of September (Michaelmas), it was time for Gage to leave Chiapa for the City of Guatemala.

On the way, he had an alarming experience.

In the town of Chimaltenango, in the highlands of Guatemala, he stayed with a certain Dominican friar named

Alonso Hidalgo, an old man who wore spectacles, and had false teeth of lead, both facts worthy of note in those days. Hidalgo was a bitter man, and an ambitious one. Though he had been born in Spain, he had been raised in Guatemala, and it was in Guatemala that he had taken his vows. He had become more Creole than the Creoles; he hated all who came from Spain, and it was his hope that, with the help of his Creole friends, he would become the Provincial. It was because of his native sourness and suspicion, Gage tells us, that he conceived the peculiar notion that Gage was a spy.

On the way to Chimaltenango, on a dangerous mountain track, Gage's mule had thrown him, and both mule and rider had rolled down the almost perpendicular incline. They would have been smashed on the rocks below, had not a shrub broken Gage's fall, and a tree the mule's. The Indians who were escorting him at once cried out *milagro, milagro*, 'miracle, miracle', and *santo, santo*, 'a saint, a saint'. The word preceded them along the road, and when they reached the next town, Gage was welcomed as a man of unusual sanctity. His impatience at being so honoured was taken by the Indians as merely an instance of his humility, and therefore a confirming indication of his holiness. In the town of Joyabaj, he sat in a special chair in the choir of the church: all the Indians of the town came up to render him homage, and to offer gifts of coins, honey, eggs, fruit and fowls. Gage, most embarrassed, asked the friar who ministered to them, one Juan Vidal, to disabuse the natives of this notion, something he could not do himself, since he possessed only a partial knowledge of their language. Instead, the friar addressed the natives to thank them 'for the great love they had shown unto an ambassador of God'.

Later, when Vidal totted up the take, he expressed his

gratitude to Gage, who had filled his larder for many days. Gage's cash reward for almost having broken his neck was forty reals, and Vidal gave him twenty more for the food offerings, which were, Gage tells us with some resentment, worth at least forty. He also gave Gage some friendly advice: such simple-minded errors should not be discouraged; for so long as the Indians thought the friars to be on the very brink of divinity, so long would they obey them in everything, so that their persons and fortunes could be commanded at pleasure.

Gage's reputation as a holy man had also preceded him to Chimaltenango; but Hidalgo's reception was cold. He simply refused to believe that anybody who came from Spain could be a saint, much less a man from England, that country of heretics. Rather, he thought, Gage must be a spy, come to view the riches of Guatemala, and afterwards betray them to England. There were, after all, many treasures in the Dominican cloister at Chimaltenango, notably a picture of Our Lady and an expensive lamp, and Gage would, he had no doubt, inquire into these. To this Gage answered in the only possible way, with a joke. He would first take notice, he said, of the pictures, tapestries, and rich cabinets in Hidalgo's chamber. He might even tell the English about Hidalgo's teeth, in which case they would make him drink very hot soup, to see if they were indeed lead, and not silver. This would certainly cause them to melt, and run down his throat. After a number of such agreeable pleasantries, 'he perceived I jeered him, and so he let me alone'.

He did not stay for supper under the roof of the suspicious old man, but set out again for Guatemala City. There, he said, he would have a light supper in the Dominican friary.

What Gage did not know then—probably he never did know—was that an order respecting him had been sent out in that year of 1627 to the Guatemalan Provincial. It had come from the Master General of the Dominican Order in Rome. It had ordered that Gage be sent to Spain 'as our English brethren need his services for the propagation of the faith'. But the order had not reached its destination. Gage was to be in the Dominican friary at Guatemala for the next three years.

XIII—*The Highland Mayans*

On his way to Guatemala, Gage would be passing through the country of the highland Mayans—the Quichés, Zutuhils, Cakchiquels, Pokomans and other related peoples. Since these peoples are not as well known as those of the valley of Mexico or the lowland Mayan area, and since Gage would be spending some time among them, it might be worth-while to say something about their history. We are fortunate in possessing a good deal of aboriginal Quiché and Cakchiquel literature, which was written down in the native languages by literate Indians shortly after the conquest, and later translated into Spanish and other European languages. The best-known of these treasures is the *Popol Vuh*, a collection of mythical and historical legends of the Quichés.

The Quichés, and the peoples related to them, were at one time under the control of the Toltec empire; indeed, they resided at this time near the great city of Tula, in the Valley of Mexico. Tula was the capital of a militaristic empire which had arisen, centuries before the Aztecs, on the ruins of the theocratic empire of Teotihuacan. Up to this time, the peoples we are discussing seem to have been bar-barians. Under the rule of the Toltecs, to whom they paid tribute, and under whom they served as mercenary soldiers, they became civilized.

Eventually they left Tula, setting out to conquer distant lands, and establish an empire of their own. First they attempted to conquer the Nonoualcas and Xulpiti of Southern Vera Cruz and Tabasco; but, while they had some success in this venture, they were eventually defeated by those who lived in the city of Zuyva. This 'formidable city' (to quote their chronicles) was located, according to some interpreters of these stories, on an island in the Laguna de Terminos in Campeche. Disorganized and depressed (*The Annals of the Cakchiquels* says 'we stripped off our feathers and we took off our ornaments'), they gave up their attempt to conquer the rich coastal area, and pushed up into what are now the Guatemalan highlands.

Here they employed Toltec methods of conquest: the use of human sacrifice to inspire terror (a device which the Aztecs used to the point of systematic atrocity), the performance of conjuring tricks which made the unsophisticated villagers think they possessed magic powers, and the more prosaic military arts of fortress-building and road-making. Once they had conquered the local peoples, they decided to legitimize their rule by sending emissaries to the two centres of Toltec rule at that time: the empire had split, and there was one centre in Yucatan, and one in the Valley of Mexico. They were, in effect, accepting the overlordship of the Toltecs, in exchange for Toltec recognition of their conquests. The emissary to Mexico apparently accomplished nothing. But the emissary to Yucatan returned with the insignia of Toltec royalty—the canopied throne, the royal flutes and drums, the feathered banners and head-dresses, and the jaguar claws.

Now, their sovereignty over the natives confirmed, the

conquerors fell to warring among themselves. By the time the Spaniards arrived, the Quichés and Cakchiquels were masters of the Guatemalan highlands, almost half of present-day Guatemala, and the Quichés were beginning to dominate the Cakchiquels.

Although their language belonged to the Mayan stock, the culture they established was Toltec in most of its essentials, with some admixture of elements from the Mayan lowlands, and from other Mexican cultures such as those of the Mixtecs and Zapotecs. The capital of the Quichés, Utatlán, had, the conquistadores tell us, twenty-four large stone houses in which the nobles dwelt. Each of these houses consisted of a large single room with a straw roof, raised on a platform about two yards from the ground, with a portico in front, and they were built around small court-yards, so that they faced each other. In these court-yards were held their religious dances. There was also, in the town centre, the palace of the ruling family, a pyramid temple, and a court for the ceremonial ball-game, which, like the tournaments of the European Middle Ages, was reserved for the nobility. To the conquistadores the architecture appeared pleasing, but undistinguished; and the sculpture was crude, compared to the beautiful stonework of the more highly civilized areas. It seems to have been a provincial variant of the great ceremonial centres of Mexico.

The town, which was built on a high mesa surrounded by ravines, had two entrances. One either climbed a steep staircase of twenty-five steps, or crossed a narrow causeway, laid with stones. Archaeological excavations have shown that these towns of the Guatemalan highlands had an extraordinary number of stone staircases, pyramids and buildings on high places, which made them very easy to defend against attackers.

In Gage's time there was nothing left of the old élite culture; the gods of America, like the old gods of Europe, had been conquered by Christ. No Christian can regret this: indeed, even if one were not a Christian, it would be naïve to regret it. The old civilization was tired; like other senile civilizations, it had become bloodthirsty, and was tearing the flesh of its own children between its rotting teeth. The Aztecs, like the Nazis, were a symptom of senile dementia. All over Mexico and Central America, civilization was falling to pieces. This is one reason why the Spaniards were welcomed. It is one reason, among others more exalted, why Christianity was welcomed.

But one of the unfortunate results of the conquest was that, while the terrorism and tyranny of the ruling class was destroyed, its high culture was destroyed also. Nothing was left but the ageless superstition of the Indian peasant; it was this, a force which could not be argued with, which could hardly be conquered even by the greatest and most discerning love, which the priests (and few of them were up to the task) had to cope with from day to day. It was in such an environment that Gage would be preaching the Word of God, and administering the sacraments. He would discover the tenacity of the old superstitions, and face supernatural terrors he was in no way prepared to face.

XIV—*In Santiago de Guatemala*

So renowned was Santiago de Guatemala that Gage had expected something as impressive as Mexico; but, in fact, he found himself in the city almost before he knew he was there. He did not enter through a gate, or pass over a bridge; no watch or guard stopped him with questions about where he was from, or where he was going; and he did not suspect he was in a city until he came upon a newly-built church standing near a refuse dump, with some mean houses near-by, some thatched and some tiled. He asked a passer-by what town he was in, and the answer came that he was in the City of Guatemala. The church, which was named San Sebastian, was the only parish church in the city. Otherwise, Santiago de Guatemala contained only its cathedral and the cloisters of the various orders. Farther on, Gage came to a broad street with houses on either side. Eventually, he arrived at the Dominican cloister, a proud and stately build-ing. He circled it on his mule, looking for the back entrance. When he found it, he alighted, knocked, and inquired for the Prior.

The Prior was Master Jacinto de Cabañas, who was also chief Master and Reader of Divinity in the College of St Thomas Aquinas, which was attached to the cloister. He had been brought up in the Spanish province of Asturias, which was visited by many English ships, and as a result he had become something of an Anglophile. For this reason, among others, he welcomed Gage, and promised to do all he could to assist him.

At the college, under Master Cabañas, Gage began to devote himself to serious study. He did so well that within three months he was nominated to defend, in a public debate before the entire college, a proposition on a subject which was, at that time, very controversial, and on which Master Cabañas had strong views.

The subject of debate was whether or not the Mother of the Lord had been born without the stain of original sin. The Jesuits, Franciscans, Scotists and the Spanish theologian Suárez maintained that she had been so born, that is, they upheld the doctrine of the Immaculate Conception. But the Thomists maintained, after Thomas Aquinas, that she, with all the race of man, had been born in original sin. Gage and Cabañas took the Thomist position.

The argument was in the medieval tradition of scholastic debate, which was still considered, in a neo-Hispanic culture soaked in the dark and heady wine of the Counter-Reformation, the only way to truth. A rank jungle of words and fine logical distinctions, a delicate green tracery of quibbles, sterile of fruit, but richly productive of leaf, grew up over the heads of the debaters, and in this verbal shrubbery major and minor premises sang like big and little birds.

The Jesuits stamped, clapped and shouted. They declared they were not surprised that Gage, an Englishman and born among heretics, should defend such a heresy; but they were surprised at hearing it defended by Master Cabañas, who had been born and educated in Spain, and was Chief Reader at the college.

Gage was not out to impress the Jesuits, though, but his fellow Dominicans. In this he succeeded. So impressed were they that when Michaelmas came round again, they made him a Reader of Arts at the College of St Thomas Aquinas. Gage thought enough of this honour to preserve the letters patent long after he became a Protestant minister. The document read as follows—

'Friar Juan Ximeno, Preacher General and Prior Provincial of the Province of Saint Vincent of Chiapa and Guatemala, Order of Preachers—whereas our Convent of Santo Domingo of Guatemala wanteth and standeth in need of a Reader of Arts: By these presents I do institute, name and appoint for Reader Friar Tomás de Santa Maria for the great satisfaction which I have of his sufficiency. And I command the Prior of the aforesaid our convent, that he put him in full possession and enjoyment of the said office. And for the greater merit of obedience, and under a formal precept, In the name of the Father, and of the Son and of the Holy Ghost, Amen. Dated in this our Convent of Chiapa la Real, the 9. of Feb. 1627. And I command these to be sealed with the great seal of our office.

Friar Juan   By the command of our
or   Reverend Father Friar
Ximeno Pal.   Juan de Santo Domingo
                          Notary

I notified these letters patent, unto the contained in them the 12. day of the month of April, 1627.
Friar Juan Batista Por.'

Not everybody was as pleased by Gage's promotion as he was. The Creole party was much offended at seeing such an honour bestowed on a newcomer to the province. This opposition, though, and the support of his *gachupine* friends, only made him the more eager in the pursuit of learning, that he might fulfil the expectations which his best friends had of him. Like the other friars, he was expected to rise at six; but in the three years he was in that convent, he would often, sustained by a cup of hot chocolate, study until one or two in the morning. Indeed, he was reluctant to preach or to hear confessions, lest his studies be interrupted.

His superiors did not allow him to remain in seclusion very long. Impressed by his eloquence and learning, they demanded that he get out and preach. He was licensed to preach in the churches of the valley, that valley of Guatemala which was, as he discovered when he emerged blinking from his cell, most beautiful.

But first we should look at the beauties of the cloister in which he had lived for three years.

It was a rich convent, drawing its revenues (thirty

thousand ducats a year net) from a water-mill, a maize-farm, a ranch, a sugar plantation, a silver mine, and several Indian towns. Before the high altar in the church there was a picture of the Virgin worked in silver, a saint's statue with six lamps of silver burning before it, and another silver lamp which was so heavy that it took three men to pull it up with a rope. The treasure of the church and cloister, Gage estimated, was worth in sum a hundred thousand ducats.

A wide walk ran before the church, and this connected the college to the cloister. In the cloister there was a spacious garden: here there were two ponds, stocked with fish and visited by water-fowl, in which a fountain played continually. There were two other gardens, one of which contained a pond, surrounded by a wall and paved at the bottom, which was a quarter of a mile long. Here there was a boat for the friars' recreation; they would often fish from it, since this pond was also well stocked with fish.

Next to the friary was the convent of the Conception, and here there dwelt a young nun who was the wonder of the city, as much for her wit and accomplishments as for her beauty. Her name was Sor Juana de Maldonado y Paz, and she was the daughter of a judge. Sor Juana was particularly noted for her ability to invent verses *ex tempore*, a talent which greatly charmed the Bishop. She was clearly his favourite, and he was trying his best to make her the abbess, in spite of the opposition of the older sisters.

She was her father's only child, and the judge had spared no money in the adorning of her apartments. Thus she had rich and costly cabinets faced with gold and silver. The religious paintings in her rooms were set in black ebony frames with gold and silver corners, and her statues of saints glittered with jewels. Her private chapel, which was hung with tapestries, had an altar decked with jewels, candlesticks,

crowns and lamps, and covered by a canopy embroi-
dered with gold. In her closet or parlour she had a small
organ and a number of other musical instruments: here,
sometimes alone and sometimes in consort with her best
friends among the nuns, she would entertain the Bishop
with music. Eventually her father built her a new set of
apartments, containing rooms, galleries and a private garden walk, and he assigned six negro maids to wait upon
her.

As to the city, it was, as we have seen, not very large. The
city proper consisted of some five thousand families, and
attached to it was an Indian suburb of about two hundred
families. It was a fairly new town. The old capital, Ciudad
Vieja, which was about three miles away, had been destroyed by flood in 1542: one of the two volcanoes near the
city was split apart by an earthquake, and the water of a
lake in its crater came rushing down on the city, inundating
it, and destroying many of the houses. The capital was removed to the city in which Gage now was: Santiago de
Guatemala, or Antigua, as it is called today. The river,
which still flowed from the mountain, now fed the orchards
and gardens of the valley.

The other volcano was still active, and the city was often
shaken by earth tremors, especially in the summer. Once,
before Gage had come, it had spewed out burning embers
and shot out boulders the size of a house, killing all the
vegetation around its sides and foot. On another occasion,
it had burned so intensely for three days and nights that
Master Cabañas had been able to read a letter in its glare,
though it was dark, and the volcano was three miles from the
city. But Gage had learned to live with the volcano, and
fears of earthquake and eruption did not mar his pleasure
in the city and its surrounding countryside.

The valley was rich and fertile. Small towns and villages crept halfway up the mountains which enclosed the narrow valley: roses and lilies bloomed all year round, and the trees were heavy with sweet and delicate fruits. The cattle were so numerous that they were slaughtered for their hides, which were shipped to Spain. The beef, Gage tells us, was good, though inferior to that of England: it sold at thirteen pounds and a half for the equivalent of threepence, between one-sixth and one-seventh of the English price of the day. At one fair which Gage attended cattle were sold at nine shillings a head; and there were so many wild cattle (or *cimarrones*) abroad that hunting parties were organized to kill them, simply to prevent their damaging the crops.

There were a number of wealthy merchants in the city; but five were notably rich, being worth about five hundred thousand ducats each. Of these five merchants, one, Antonio Justiniano, was 'Genoese born'; and two were Spaniards. The other two were 'Portuguese', thus, in all probability, Jews: Jews in Spanish possessions commonly referred to themselves, and were referred to, as 'Portuguese'. The names of these latter two were Antonio Fernández and Bartolomé Nuñez, 'whereof the first in my time departed from Guatemala for some reasons which here I must conceal'.

This is one of the most mysterious statements in Gage's book. Why should he conceal Fernández' reasons for departure? He conceals nothing else about the people he met in the New World: indeed, he gleefully expands on their peccadilloes and oddities. He owed no special debt of gratitude to Fernández, or at least he mentions none. His silence can hardly be due to shame. Had Fernández' departure been connected in some way with an incident which showed Gage himself in a discreditable light, he would probably not have mentioned it. The phrase 'for some reasons which here I must conceal' can hardly fail to suggest political or religious intrigue, and that of a kind involving England, since otherwise there could hardly have been a motive to 'conceal' the 'reasons' in a book published in England. And he adds, even more mysteriously, 'The other four I left there, the three of them living at that end of the city called *Barrio de Santo Domingo*, or the Street of St Dominic, whose houses and presence makes that street excel all the rest of the city, and their wealth and trading were enough to denominate Guatemala a very rich city.' Why is he so careful to indicate where their houses are to be found? He does not give us specific addresses in his description of any other city. This is specially interesting in view of the fact that his entire description of Guatemala is clearly intended to be of use to an invading army: Gage was later to propose to Cromwell that mainland America be invaded through that province. There is an oddity about the whole business, which is discussed in an appendix to this book.

The description, which is as detailed as Baedeker, need not be recapitulated in detail; but among the careful descriptions are some good stories which, among other things, give an excellent idea of the state of the negroes, or, as Gage calls them, the Blackamoors.

A number of escaped slaves—called *cimarrones* after the Spanish term for wild cattle—roamed the woods and mountains. Like the Maroons of Jamaica, they were organized loosely into bands, and, like them, they waged occasional war against the settlements. Usually, though, they confined themselves to attacks on mule-trains; and their methods were rather gallant and Robin Hoodish: they took only the goods they needed, and never harmed those escorting the trains unless they retaliated with force. It was an intelligent policy: as a rule, the escorts of the mule-trains gave them what they wanted without fighting, and often the slaves in the caravans ran away and joined them.

Not all the negroes were slaves. Some were free men, and a few had prospered. There was one, at a place called El Agua Caliente, who was rich in cattle, sheep and goats, and particularly well-known for his excellent cheeses. It was commonly felt that he could not have become so wealthy simply by running an efficient farm: he was, after all, only a negro, and could thus have had no head for business. It was believed that he had found some hidden treasure. He was summoned by the Chancery Court of Guatemala, to reveal the source of his income; but his answer was disappointing: he merely said that when he had been young and a slave, he had been fortunate enough to have a kind master, who had allowed him to make money on his own; that he had, by the exercise of thrift and prudence, accumulated enough money to buy his freedom, and after that a small house with some livestock; and that from that moment God had prospered him.

Clearly this was an unusual case. Few slaves had such kindly masters, though few had masters so cruel as the man we are about to describe.

One of Gage's friends was a miser named Juan Palomeque He was worth six hundred thousand ducats, but he lived like a peasant on milk, curds, hard biscuit and jerked beef. Though he owned good houses in the capital, he dwelt among his slaves, in a poor thatched house little better than a hut. He was a cruel and vicious man. When he saw, in the streets of the city, an attractive female slave whose bearing indicated that she still retained a degree of personal pride, he would purchase her so that he might degrade her with enforced debauchery. In this he was no miser: in order to buy a female slave who had strongly aroused this obscene itch to kill the soul, he would frequently pay much more than she was worth in the market. He destroyed the pride of his male slaves in a different way, by sleeping with their wives. He took great pleasure in torturing his male slaves, and, here again, he concentrated on those who showed independence of spirit. One of these, whose slave-name was Macao, he would hang up by the arms, whipping him until his back was a mass of red flesh; then, as a salve, he would pour boiling grease over the wounds. He had branded Macao with irons on his face, hands, arms, back, belly, thighs and legs. Such tortures were forbidden, of course, by the Spanish laws governing the treatment of slaves.

As to Gage's role in the matter—and he does not seem to have felt that more was demanded of him—he did take it upon him to counsel Macao against hanging himself. The word 'friend', applied to Palomeque, is Gage's own.

So far as the Indians were concerned—'The condition of the Indians of this country of Guatemala is as sad and as much to be pitied as of any Indians in America, for that I may say it is with them, in some sort, as it was with Israel in Egypt. Though it is true there ought not to be any comparison made between the Israelites and the Indians, those being God's people, these not as yet—' Palomeque had himself killed two Indians, and had bought himself off at the trial, as if he had killed two dogs.

It is not news, of course, that the Indians and negroes suffered under the Spaniards. It is common to blame Spain and the Roman Church for such horrors. Yet it is clear that the real culprits were the Creole landlords, and the merchants who dealt in slaves and dominated the sugar industry, in which the worst abuses occurred. The business headquarters of the slave trade was, after all, in Amsterdam, not Seville or Cadiz. Spanish law relating to Negro slavery was cruel enough, in the sense that slavery itself is cruel; but it did not sanction atrocities. The laws relating to Indians were less cruel; indeed, they might be described as 'paternalistic'. Had not the King, in 'The New Laws for the Good Treatment and Preservation of the Indians', promulgated in 1542, declared of the Indians—'we wish them to be treated as our subjects of the Crown of Spain, for that they are'? And had not Pope Paul III said in a Bull of 1537 that they were inspired by the devil, who claimed 'that the Indians of the West and the South, and other people of whom we have recent knowledge, should be treated as dumb brutes created for our service, pretending that they are incapable of receiving the Catholic faith'?; and in this same Bull he refers to racist doctrine as 'never before heard of'.

Spain might be accused, with some justification, of a quixotic archaism. In her Indian laws, she was attempting to transplant the feudal system, already out of date in Europe, to America. The concept was not unfamiliar to the Indians: the Aztec lords had been something between imperial bureaucrats and feudal lords. But the Creole *encomenderos*, newly-created 'aristocrats', did not understand the obligations of the lord to his serf, obligations which, when they were honoured, made feudalism tolerable in the main, and in some cases, better than tolerable. They only saw that they had been given the right to exploit the labour of others. The spirit of rapacity and 'free enterprise', still largely expressed in an agricultural and mercantile rather than a manufacturing economy, was growing. The Spanish Crown resisted the trend: in the eighteenth century, for example, the Crown established a forty-eight-hour work week in the mines, and granted to the miners a profit based on a percentage of the ore mined. A new class, though, was springing up in the New World—a class of sugar-planters, mine-owners, owners of textile factories and workshops of all descriptions, and slave-traders: there was only one way to make money and rise in the world, and that was to participate, more or less enthusiastically, in a moral climate whose two extremes were petty venality and atrocity. If the court and church were to blame it was because, in spite of their attempts to be just, they could not resist the wealth pouring in from the New World. Complaining bitterly of the cruelty and dishonesty of their subjects and adherents, they averted their eyes, and held out their hands, palms uppermost, to receive the money made by the practices they professed to abhor. They had been compromised by the sordid demands of empire: had they attempted to enforce fully the laws they had promulgated, there would have been a Creole revolution, and Spain, deprived of the treasure of the New World, would have gone bankrupt.

Thus, though the enslavement of Indians was forbidden by law, they were often treated as slaves. Gage had ministered to some whose pay had been many blows, a few wounds, and little or no wages. These had 'sullenly and stubbornly' laid down on their beds, and starved themselves to death.

'The Spaniards that live about that country (especially the farmers of the Valley of Mixco, Pinola, Petapa, Amatitlán, and those of the Sacatepéquez) allege that all their trading and farming is for the good of the commonwealth, and therefore, whereas there are not Spaniards enough for so ample and large a country to do all their work, and all are not able to buy slaves and Blackamoors, they stand in need of the Indians' help to serve them for their pay and hire; whereupon it hath been considered that a partition of Indian labourers be made every Monday, or Sunday in the afternoon to the Spaniards, according to the farms they occupy, or according to their several employments, calling, and trading with mules, or any other way. So that for such and such a district there is named an officer, who is called *juez repartidor*, who according to a list made of every farm, house and person, is to give so many Indians by the week. And here is a door opened to the President of Guatemala, and to the judges, to provide well for their menial servants, whom they commonly appoint for this office, which is thus performed by them. They name the town and place of their meeting upon Sunday or Monday, to the which themselves and the Spaniards of that district do resort. The Indians of the several towns are to have in readiness as many labourers as the Court of Guatemala hath appointed to be weekly taken out of such a town. These are conducted by an Indian officer to the town of general meeting, and when they come thither with their tools, their spades, shovels, bills, or axes, with their provisions of victuals for a week (which are commonly some dry cakes of maize, puddings of *frijoles*, or French beans, and a little chile or biting long pepper, or a bit of cold meat for the first day or two) and with beds on their backs (which is only a coarse woollen mantle to wrap about them when they lie on the bare ground), then they are shut up in the town-house, some with blows, some with spurning, some with boxes on the ear, if presently they go not in.

'Now all being gathered together, and the house filled with them, the *juez repartidor*, or officer, calls by the order of the list such and such a Spaniard, and also calls out of the house so many Indians as by the Court are commanded to be given him (some are allowed three, some four, some ten, some fifteen, some twenty, according to their employments) and delivereth unto the Spaniard his Indians, and so to all the rest, till they be all served; who when they receive their Indians, take from them a tool, or their mantles, to secure them that they run not away; and for every Indian delivered unto them, they give unto the *juez repartidor*, or officer, half a real, which is threepence an Indian for his fees, which mounteth yearly to him to a great deal of money, for some officers make a partition or distribution of four hundred, some of two hundred, some of three hundred Indians every week, and carrieth home with him so many half hundred reals for one or half a day's work. If complaint be made by any Spaniard that such and such an Indian did run away from him, and served him not the week past, the Indian must be brought, and surely tied to a post by his hands in the market-place, and there be whipped upon his bare back. But if the poor Indian complain that the Spaniards cozened and cheated him of his shovel, axe, bill, mantle, or wages, no justice shall be executed against the cheating Spaniard, neither shall the Indian be righted, though it is true the order runs equally in favour of both Indian and Spaniard.'

The arrangement was, in fact, a *corvée*, or work tax. It might be compared to the *corvée* of seigneurial Quebec, and was not, in itself, any less just than our own money taxes. True, the average Indian would work on *corvée* three or four weeks in the year, as compared to three or four days for the average *censitaire*, or peasant, in Quebec. On the other hand, he was paid, while the *censitaire* was not. The Indian would be paid roughly half a crown for six days' work, a wage which appears ridiculous to us, but which, in terms of the purchasing power of money at that time, was not at all ridiculous, though it was small. For example, English agricultural labourers were receiving, at that time, weekly wages of from three to five shillings. Thus Indians were receiving half the high English rate and more than two-thirds of the low; and it must be remembered that the price of beef in Guatemala was one sixth to one-seventh of the English price.

Again we find that the laws of the Spanish Crown, which fixed the wages and attempted to regulate the working conditions of the Indians, were by no means unjust. This point cannot be over-stressed if we are to understand Gage's Mexico. The trouble did not lie in the law, but in the fact that the Creoles broke the law whenever possible. The

Spanish Crown had envisioned what might be called an enlightened feudalism, which was quite in the spirit of its archaising idealism: the Creoles turned it into a system approaching chattel slavery.

Some Spaniards, who did not have a full week's work for their Indians to do, would take advantage of their desire to return to the poor comforts of their homes; they would work them for half a week, and then say, 'What will you give me now, if I let you go home to do your own work?' Often the Indians would pay them for this privilege. Thus the land-owners would find themselves, after the Indians had gone, with their work done, and a small financial gain as well.

Some would whip the Indians for working too slow, or would wound them with their swords if they were rash enough to complain about their treatment. Some were even contemptible enough to confiscate their tools. Others would visit the wives of those who were assigned to them. Indian carriers—who sometimes carried loads of over a hundred-weight for a two- or three-day journey—would frequently be sent home, at the end of the journey, with no pay but blows, their masters having picked a quarrel with them to avoid payment.

There had been, and would be, insurrections, but they did not succeed. The imperialist principle of the *roi nègre* was applied with some skill. The descendants of the indigenous kings and nobles had their places among the minor gentry; the village chiefs were allowed to exploit their fellow-Indians in small ways; Indians with a sense of vocation or an intellectual bent were absorbed into the lower levels of the church hierarchy; and there was nothing to prevent an Indian's achieving a modest success as a farmer, rancher, or petty merchant. Thus potential leaders were diverted into working hard for small if real rewards. No Indian could carry arms, not even a bow and arrows; even a patent or nobility did not, as a rule, give him the right to carry a sword. Furthermore, the priests and friars calmed them whenever they were disposed to mutiny, persuading them to bear and suffer all for God's sake and the good of the Commonwealth.

The Indians had another consolation, and that was drink. '... if they can get any drink that will make them mad drunk, they will not give it over as long as a drop is left or a penny remains in their purse to purchase it.' They made their own *chicha*, and would go to insane lengths to strengthen it so that it would bring on the desired oblivion. In some towns they would put a live toad in the jar and close it up until the toad was thoroughly consumed. Once, in the town of Mixco, Gage and some officers of justice raided a house in which the Indians were drinking, and discovered four unopened jars of this liquor. When they were broken, and the contents were poured out in the street, the stink was such that Gage vomited on the spot.

They were, in fact, becoming 'drunken Indians'. The descendants of the war-like Tenochcas, the learned Texcocans, the subtle Mayans were being driven, melted and crushed down into that same state of clownish debauchery into which the tribes of North America would later fall. Out of a number of extraordinarily varied cultures and ethnic groups, the European was creating 'the Indian'. Certainly, drink had become to the natives—as narcotics have become to some of the negroes of the United States ghettos, as opium became to the Chinese coolie class in the decadence of the Chinese Empire, as marijuana, LSD and sexual drifting have become to many gentle and sensitive persons of all races in the United States—a way of escape from an intolerable situation. Certain Creoles were glad to help them escape. In spite of a law forbidding the sale of wine in Indian communities, there were a number of pedlars going from town to town, selling diluted wine strengthened with cheap and dangerous drugs. The local authorities turned their heads the other way, as they did in British Columbia in the 1860's, when the Indians were being poisoned or driven mad by a solution of red pepper in diluted alcohol, a drink from which a number of fortunes were made.

XV—*An Attempted Journey to Yucatan*

FOR three years Gage read in arts at the College of Guatemala. The more he studied, the more he became convinced that Roman Catholic theology was full of 'lies, errors, falsities and superstitions'. He was going through one of the typical crises of his time. He was becoming a Protestant. But in seventeenth-century Mexico, it was dangerous to be a Protestant: one might be burned at the stake.

The points which chiefly troubled him were seven: the transubstantiation of the consecrated elements during the sacrifice of the Mass, the existence of Purgatory, the merit of man's works, free will, the priest's power to absolve from sin, the entire complex of beliefs and ritual practices associated with the saints and the Virgin Mary, and the infallibility o the Pope and his council—which last point, while it was not a dogma as yet, was often treated as if it was. In addition to these theological doubts, which might have assailed him anywhere, he was troubled by the greed, luxury and toleration of evil and oppression which he had found in the Mexican Church. Certainly, he may have been homesick as well. Yet we have no reason to question the sincerity of his doubts, or to deny that study, even of Roman Catholic authors alone, might well have strengthened them.

His doubts also strengthened his desire to return to England. He knew, he says, that there 'many things were held contrary to the Church of Rome, but what particulars they were I could not tell, not having been brought up in the Protestant church, and having been sent young over to St Omer'. Yet, while he wishes us to believe that he learned nothing of Protestant theology during this time, the evidence is that he was becoming acquainted with it.

He addressed petitions to his Provincial and to the President of Guatemala, asking that he might be allowed to return to Spain, there to be posted to the English mission. An order to this effect had, as we have seen, been sent from Rome; but it had not reached its destination. Gage's petition was rejected. There was an inflexible rule that all priests sent to the Indies must stay there ten years.

Gage therefore decided to request permission that he be allowed to leave the cloister, and become a priest in one of the Indian towns. It is clear enough that he intended, by delicately fleecing his parishioners, to make enough money to enable him to buy his passage home. Thus poor Gage, tempted by necessity and strong desire, celebrated his liberation from the chains of Roman Catholicism by rushing to embrace the same sin he had, up to then, so roundly condemned. At the same time, he wrote to a 'friend' in San Lucar in Spain, asking him to obtain a licence from the Court and from the General of the Order at Rome, which would assign him to England. The 'friend' was that same 'old crab-faced English friar', Pablo de Londres, who had tried to prevent his going to the Philippines in the first place.

Now at this time Friar Francisco Morán, Prior of Cobán in the Province of Vera Paz, was petitioning the President

and Chancery of Guatemala for assistance in the discovery
of a route from Guatemala into Yucatan. Many of the
Indians there were still heathen, and had been attacking
villages of Christian Indians. Morán was a friend of Gage;
they had both studied, though at different times, in the
cloister of San Pablo de Valladolid. Morán persuaded Gage
to accompany him on this journey, in which many heathen
would be converted, and, no doubt, much treasure discovered. 'I was not hard to be persuaded', says Gage with
stupefying unctuousness, 'being above all desirous to convert to Christianity a people that had never heard of Christ;
and so purposed to forsake that honour which I had in the
University, in order to make Christ known unto that heath-
enish people.'

When they left, they took with them some money and gifts
for the Indians, and an escort of fifty armed Spaniards. At
the towns of San Pedro and San Juan, they added one
hundred Indians to the party. For two days they travelled
comfortably on mule-back, moving from one small Christian
village to another; but as they approached the borders of
Christian settlement, the roads turned to paths, and the
paths narrowed and were blurred with grass, and finally
melted into forest. Now their mules could not help them.
They left them on the edge of the forest, and proceeded on
foot.

For two days they moved up and down the slopes of
wooded mountains, pushing through thickets and stumbling
over rocks and fallen trees. At night they mounted a guard,
but there were neither friends nor enemies to be seen. They
found wild fruits in the mountains, and in the valleys and
hollows, where the springs and brooks were, they found cacao
and achiote trees. On the third day they came on a low
valley with a shallow river running through it, and here they

found a few maize-fields. They drew together, and kept careful watch as they travelled.

Suddenly—and such discoveries can be very sudden in deep forest—they stumbled on a tiny hamlet of half a dozen thatched huts. Most of the inhabitants were away: they found only two men, three women, and five young children. When the Indians saw the Spaniards they began to weep aloud and cry for mercy. At this, Morán, who had a smattering of their language, tried to comfort them, and the Spaniards gave them some food and clothing. The Indians were forced to accompany the expedition, the hope being that they would lead the Spaniards to a treasure, or another village at least; but they refused to speak a word.

Later, they found some human tracks, and they followed them through the forest until they came, near dusk, to another hamlet, this time consisting of a dozen huts. It contained about twenty men, women and children. The expedition confiscated their bows and arrows, ate up most of their stock of plantains, fish and venison, and rested there the night. The next day they sent out some scouts, who returned to say that they had found other huts and garden plots, but no Indians, because they had all fled into the forest.

The next day they moved forward again, heading for a group of plantations which were, their scouts told them, in open country; here they could move more easily, and see more clearly any dangers—human or animal—which threatened them. They were moving along the river bank from one tiny village to another. It was hot and humid, and they were beginning to weaken with fevers and dysentery. Now their prisoners grew more communicative: there was some gold, they said, in the river, and farther on there was a great lake. There were many thousands of Indians living on its shores, and they were very warlike, and good bowmen.

Some of the more bellicose members of the expedition were encouraged by this move; many, however, began to murmur against Morán, who had brought them so far and placed them in such great danger.

At midnight, as the Spaniards were sleeping—most of them in hammocks, but some on the ground—the watch gave the alarm. Enemies were approaching, to the number, they estimated, of about a thousand. The Spaniards and their Indian allies began to beat their drums and fire off their muskets and fowling-pieces; and at this the attacking Indians, scattered through the trees, gave their war-cries, 'which up-roar and sudden affrightment', says Gage, 'added sweat and fear to my fever'.

Morán had come to him to confess, which did not make him feel any better. But Morán comforted Gage as best he could: there was, he said, little they could do; the soldiers were around the camp in a ring formation, and they would be wiser to stay where they were, in which case they might well survive, than to attempt to flee, which would certainly result in death.

As it happened, the skirmish did not last longer than an hour. The attackers disappeared into the night-bound forest, leaving ten of their number behind as prisoners. In the morning, the Spaniards found thirteen of their attackers dead on the ground. Five of the defenders were wounded, but only one of them fatally: he died of his wounds the next day.

Later the prisoners were questioned. They answered in a spirit of noble defiance. If the Spaniards did not go away, they said, six or seven thousand would come against them. They added that they were well aware that the Spaniards controlled the country round about them; all they wanted was the little portion which they now had. Their only desire was to live there in peace. If the Spaniards wished to see their country, and pass through it as friends, they were welcome; but if they came to fight and enslave the people, as their neighbours had been enslaved, they would die fighting rather than yield.

There was much debate among the soldiers. Some, with Morán, felt they should take the Indians at their word, and go peaceably through their country until they came to Yucatan; others thought they should fight; others argued in favour of turning back. Nothing was agreed upon that day; but they could not move, in any case, because of the sick and wounded. That night the Indians gathered around the camp again, but disappeared when they saw the Spaniards were waiting for them. In the morning they decided to turn back, but not until Morán had asked the Indians if they would let him return later, and pass through their country to Yucatan. If they agreed, he said, he would come with no more than half a dozen Indians, and would place his life in their hands. They answered that this was quite acceptable to them.

The next year, Gage tells us, he did return, as he had promised, and passed through to Yucatan without incident.

But now they turned back, retracing their steps, and as they went Gage's fever began to leave him. With them they carried some of the Indian children they had seized in the villages. These were baptized in Cobán, and assigned to Dominican cloisters, where they would be brought up as Christians.

'I remained after this for a while in Cobán, and in the towns about, until such a time as the ships came to the gulf; whither I went with Morán to buy wines, oil, iron, cloth and such things as the cloister wanted for the present. At which time there being a frigate ready to depart to Trujillo (some occasions drawing Morán thither) I took ship with him. We stayed not much above a week in that port (which is a weak one, as the English and Hollanders taking of it can witness) but presently we thought of returning back to Guatemala by land through the country of Comayagua, commonly called Honduras. This is a woody and mountainous country, very bad and inconvenient for travellers, and besides very poor; there the commodities are hides, *cañafistula*, and *zarzaparrilla*, and such want of bread that about Trujillo they make use of what they call *cassave*, which is a dry root that being eaten dry doth choke, and therefore is soaked in broth, water, wine, or chocolate, that so it may go down. Within the country, and especially about the city of Comayagua (which is a bishop's seat, though a small place of some five hundred inhabitants at the most) there is more store of maize by reason of some Indians, who are gathered to towns, few and small. I found this country one of the poorest in all America. The chief place in it for health and good living is the valley which is called Gracias á Dios, there are some rich farms of cattle and wheat; but it lieth as near to the country of Guatemala as to Comayagua, and on this side the ways are better than on that, therefore, more of that wheat is transported to Guatemala and to the towns about it than to Comayagua or Trujillo. From Trujillo to Guatemala there are between four score and a hundred leagues, which we travelled by land, not wanting in a barren country, neither guides nor provision, for the poor Indians thought neither their personal attendance nor anything that they enjoyed too good for us.

'Thus we came again to Guatemala, and were by the friars joyfully entertained, and by the President highly rewarded, and by the city called true Apostles, because we had ventured our lives for the discovery of heathens, and opened a way for their conversion, and found out the chief place of their residence, and sent before us those children to the city who witnessed with being in the cloister our pains and endeavours.'

XVI—*Mixco and Pinola*

THE journey to the border of Yucatan had been an adventure; but there had been no treasure, and Gage had not raised one real towards his fare home. He therefore fell back on his original plan: he decided to take advantage of the opportunities in the Indian towns around the City of Guatemala.

He managed to obtain a licence which made him resident priest in the towns of Mixco and Pinola. In these towns, and in the neighbouring towns of Petapa and Amatitlán, the Indians spoke Pokoman, a dialect of the Mayan language.

Thus, two weeks before Midsummer Day in 1630, he went to the town of Petapa, six leagues from Santiago de Guatemala, and set to work studying Pokoman under Friar Pedro Molina, who was well versed in the language, and was now too old to carry out his duties without assistance. First, Molina schooled Gage in the rudiments of the language, then he put him to work for a fortnight declining nouns and conjugating verbs. Vocabulary followed, and oral work. After six weeks of this kind of study, Molina gave him some sermons to translate. By Michaelmas, in a little over a quarter of a year, Gage felt confident enough to preach to the Indians on his own, and Molina was sufficiently pleased with his progress to recommend that he be assigned his own parish.

The towns of Mixco and Pinola, which he was to serve, were governed from the cloister in Guatemala, as were all the towns in the valley. Gage was enjoined to submit a quarterly account to the cloister, which was entitled to all

NOVA MEXICO

Mexico City in the mid-seventeenth century—an English conception

A religious procession in Mexico City, 1663

The viceroy's palace in Mexico City

moneys collected, after the resident priest had deducted his living expenses.

The sums involved were not inconsiderable. First, and perhaps least, each of the two towns had a common piece of land, sown with wheat or maize, whose profits were set aside for the priest, and turned over to him in monthly instalments. As for what else came in, let Gage tell of it: he kept very accurate accounts, and the figures are as illuminating to us as they were pleasing to him.

'Besides this monthly allowance, I had from the soda-lities of the souls in purgatory every week in each town two crowns for a Mass; every month two crowns in Pinola upon the first Sunday of the month from the sodality of the Rosary, and in Mixco likewise every month from three sodalities of the Rosary of the Virgin Mary, belonging to the Indians, the Spaniards and the Blackamoors, two crowns apiece. Further from two more sodalities be-longing to the Vera Cruz, or the Cross of Christ, every month two crowns apiece. And in Mixco from a sodality of the Spaniards belonging to San Nicolás de Tolentino, two crowns every month. And from a sodality of San Blas in Pinola every month two more crowns; and finally in Mixco from a sodality entitled of San Jacinto every month yet two more crowns, besides some offerings of either money, fowls or candles upon those days whereon these masses were sung; all which amounted to three score and nine crowns a month, which was surely settled and paid before the end of the month. Besides from what I have formerly said of the saints' statues which do belong unto the churches, and do there constantly bring both money, fowls, candles and other offerings upon their day unto the priest, the yearly revenues which I had in those two towns will appear not to have been small; for in Mixco there were in my time eighteen saints' images, and twenty in Pinola; which brought me upon their day four crowns apiece for Mass and sermon and procession, besides fowls, turkeys and cacao, and the offerings before the saints, which commonly might be worth at least three crowns upon every saint's day, which yearly amounted to at least two hundred three score and six crowns. Besides, the sodalities of the Rosary of the Virgin (which as I have said were four, three in Mixco and one in Pinola), upon five several feasts of the year (which are most observed by the Church of Rome) brought unto me four crowns, two for the day's Mass, and two for a Mass the day following, which they call the anniversary for the dead who had belonged unto those sodalities, which besides those days' offerings (which sometimes were more, sometimes less) and the Indians' presents of fowls and cacao, made up yearly four score crowns more. Besides this, the two sodalities of the Vera Cruz upon two feasts of the Cross, the one upon the fourteenth of September, the other upon the third of May brought four crowns apiece for the Mass of the day, and the anniversary Mass following, and upon every Friday in Lent two crowns, which in the whole year came to four and forty crowns; all of which above reckoned was as a sure rent in those two towns. But should I spend time to reckon up what besides did accidentally fall would be tedious.

'The Christmas offerings in both those two towns were worth to me when I lived there at least forty crowns. Thursday and Friday offerings before Easter Day were about a hundred crowns; All Souls' Day offerings commonly worth four score crowns; and Candlemas Day offerings commonly forty more. Besides what was offered upon the feast of each town by all the country which came in, which in Mexico one year was worth unto me in candles and money fourscore crowns, and in Pinola (as I reckoned it) fifty more. The communicants (every one giving a real) might make up in both towns at least a thousand reals; and the confessions in Lent at least a thousand more, besides other offerings of eggs, honey, cacao, fowls and fruits. Every christening brought two reals, every marriage two crowns; every one's death two crowns more at least, and some in my time died who would leave ten or twelve crowns for five or six Masses to be sung for their souls.

'Thus are those fools taught that by the priest's singing their souls are delivered from weeping, and from the fire and torments of Purgatory; and thus by singing all the year do these friars charm from the poor Indians and their sodalities and saints an infinite treasure wherewith they enrich themselves and their cloisters, as may be gathered from what I have noted by my own experience in those two towns of Mixco and Pinola, which were far inferior yet to Petapa and Amatitlán in the same valley, and not to be compared in offerings and other church duties to many other towns about that country, which yet yielded unto me with the offerings cast into the chests which stood in the churches for the souls of Purgatory, and with what the Indians offered when they came to speak unto me (for they never visit the priest with empty hands) and with what other Mass stipends did casually come in, the sum of at least two thousand crowns of Spanish money, which might yearly amount to five hundred English pounds. I thought this benefice might be a fitter place for me to live in than in the cloister of Guatemala, wearying out my brains with points of false grounded divinity to get only the applause of the scholars of the University; and now and then some small profit . . .'

Gage had made a careful study of the account books of Mixco and Pinola. He had discovered that his immediate predecessor had remitted, of the above-mentioned two thousand crowns per annum, only four hundred to the cloister in Santiago de Guatemala. Those who had preceded him had sent little more. Gage, with the most charming effrontery, proudly told his superiors he could do better: by the practice of careful economies, he could promise to give the cloister four hundred and fifty per annum. The Prior was overwhelmed by such evidence of Gage's devotion. He told him in return that he would never want for wine, but should send his order in to the cloister every month. Furthermore, he could have a complete change of clothing once a year. Gage concludes:

'And here I desire, that England take notice how a friar that hath professed to be a mendicant, being beneficed in America, may live with four hundred pounds a year clear, and some with much more, with most of his clothing given him beside, and the most charge of his wine supplied, with the abundance of fowls which cost him nothing, and with such plenty of beef as yields him thirteen pounds for threepence.'

Gage now settled down to the comfortable life of a Mexican country priest. He had two houses, one in Mixco, and one in Pinola. He does not describe them explicitly, but scattered references in his narrative give us some idea of what they were like. His house in Mixco, which adjoined the church and a garden, had the thick walls so common in Spain and its colonies, and so suited to hot climates. It had a 'long gallery', probably more like a hall than the stately room the phrase suggests. His chamber was upstairs. The house at Pinola seems to have been of one storey, with four or five rooms, a small storage room, and a garden. There were servants living in each house.

He tells us nothing of the furnishings: Gage only mentions such things when he wishes to draw attention to the extravagance of others. We must therefore assume that it was furnished in the style typical of its time and place. Seventeenth-century Mexican and Central American houses were not, as a rule, cluttered with furniture. Even principal rooms might contain only walnut chairs and cushions, with a rug on the floor and hangings on the walls. Dining-rooms were usually furnished with a wooden table and benches. A bedroom might contain a canopied bed with turned and gilded

132

columns, and those beautiful chests and coffers which were used instead of wardrobes and chests of drawers. Perhaps (we know this was the case in Gage's bedroom) there might be a writing table: wealthier persons would possess an elaborate escritoire. But though the pieces were few, they were richly worked. A massive virility of design, which in inferior pieces became a rustic heaviness, was combined with ornate surface decoration: in Mexico, not yet won over to the High Baroque style now fashionable in Spain, this carving was Renaissance, 'plateresque', in feeling. The furniture of the time had authority, if not delicacy. Each piece asserted its place in the room, and the effect, if the furniture was in the best tradition, was not one of bareness, but of a massive splendour.

Once Gage had established residence, he began to think again of ways in which he might return to England. He had become friendly with a certain Isidro de Zepeda, a Seville merchant and sea-captain who frequently passed through the valley. Gage had sent messages through him to his friends in Spain, though without much effect. Finally he threw himself on the captain's mercy, asking him to carry him in his ship to Spain. This the merchant refused to do, because of the danger it would place him in, if a complaint were made to the President of Guatemala. Rather, he told Gage, he should stay where he was, and accumulate money, so that he could return after his ten years with some wealth, and the approval of his superiors as well.

Gage was to spend five years in the towns of Mixco and Pinola. He would make a few friends, among them the 'Blackamoor' Miguel Dalva. It would be a lonely life, but not a poor one. In his time there were four great disasters, all of which proved to be of some profit to him.

In his first year there was a plague of locusts. When they came, it was in such a great cloud that they obscured the face

133

of the sun; and they hung so thick on the branches of the fruit trees that they tore them away from their trunks. Gage, riding along the highway on his mule, had to cover his face as if he were in a snow storm. Where the locusts alighted, all green disappeared. The peasants were in a continual clamour for wafers with portraits of the saints impressed upon them, and these they buried in the fields, after Gage had blessed them, to drive the locusts away. Most of the images in the Mixco church were carried in procession to the fields. One cannot expect to have miracles for nothing; and, what with the masses, the processions and the wafers, Gage did well that year.

The next year there was a plague. Ninety died in Mixco, and in Pinola over a hundred. For every person over eight years old who had died, Gage received two crowns: the money would be used to finance a Mass, which would help his soul out of Purgatory. These deaths created an economic crisis: the Creole landowners of the valley, who used the Indians as farm labourers, began to worry about the reduction of the labour force. In the true spirit of enlightened self-interest, they ordered a numbering of the people, and forced into marriage all those of twelve years or over. Gage married over eighty couples that year. Each marriage brought in a little more money.

After the plague there were great storms. Many fields and cottages were flooded, and two houses and a chapel were destroyed. The high altar at Petapa was struck by lightning, and two travellers and a friar were killed by thunderbolts. Gage's own house was struck by lightning; but though two calves in his yard were killed, and he was knocked unconscious, he escaped serious injury. To protect the people from thunderbolts, there were more processions with images of the saints—and more money for Gage.

There was an earthquake the following summer. It was not serious. But there was a great and quite justified fear of earthquakes in Guatemala, and it seemed best to bring out the images of the saints once again, in order to prevent a more serious seismic disturbance. Thus there were more processions, and more money for Gage.

Now there is no doubt that Gage—in his hatred of the Papists—does not hesitate to paint himself in dark colours, so that the Church of Rome may stand condemned in him. But it is also clear that where money was concerned, he had no scruples, provided it was obtained within the law. Where money was not concerned, he could be compassionate and understanding, even courageous. For example, he hauled a Spaniard to court for beating an Indian almost to death, and this at some risk to his own life, for the Spaniard threatened to kill him, and, indeed, went so far as to enter his yard with a naked sword. Certainly the Spaniard was apprehended, fined and imprisoned; but such acts of courage should be taken into account, when one is drawing up the balance sheet of Gage's life in Mexico.

XVII—*Witches and 'Nahualistas'*

THE Christianity of the Indians was, Gage tells us, an external thing. 'Most of the Indians', he says, 'are but formally Christians, and only outwardly appear such, but secretly are given to witchcraft and idolatry.' What had survived, it should be remembered, was not the high religion of the great civilizations, which had had its own profundity. In pagan days, the peasants and poor craftsmen had known little of the mysteries of the Mayan or Toltec religions, in which astrology, magic, the physical sciences, high philosophy, and a degree of true religious feeling were combined in a tremendous and complicated synthesis. Nor were they encouraged to investigate such matters; it was enough that the priests and lords said that such and such was so. They performed whatever roles they were assigned in the great rituals held in the ceremonial centres, and returned home to their little family shrines, to the propitiation of the spirits of game animals and domesticated plants, and to the gross and sometimes rudely beautiful rituals which had long preceded the building of the great temples, and would outlast them.

There was one element of the old civilization which the Spaniards, or any Christian people, no matter how anthropologically enlightened, would have had to suppress most rigorously, and that was human sacrifice. This would not have been difficult in itself, since much enlightened Mayan and Toltec, and even Aztec, opinion had always regarded it as a dubious, even an abominable practice. Some of the customs and rites connected with sex (such as polygamy, the phallic rituals associated with the goddess Tlazolteotl, and the licensed promiscuity of the *telpochcalli*, or schools for male commoners) were also repellent. But here again, the enlightened among the Indians also found them repellent, or at least, 'common'. Indeed, the professed sexual morality of the Aztec upper classes was harshly Puritanical, though their private practice was often—and this is hardly unusual—something else again.

Obviously, it had been no mistake to attempt to Christianize Indian culture: many of the Indians welcomed Christianity, and some looked upon its coming as a fulfilment of ancient prophecies. Nor was it a mistake to prevent such abominations as human sacrifice by force, or to use force to protect those Indians who had become Christians. The mistake, rather, lay in the attempt to destroy Indian culture

136

as a whole. For, as everybody knows, the Spaniards—except for a few missionaries whose understanding of native ways exposed them continually to charges of heresy—saw the devil in everything the Indians did. In this, the first conquerors were not unlike the Puritans of New England. They stamped out the most harmless native customs, and the high intellectual culture of the upper classes, with the same passion that they expended on the abolition of human sacrifice. As a result, the Indians themselves lost any sense of moral discrimination so far as their own culture was concerned: they either rejected it entirely, and accepted the role of half-men in a totally Spanish culture, or they clung indiscriminately to everything they could preserve, even human sacrifice, which became, almost, a symbol of cultural survival.

Thus the records of ecclesiastical and civil courts during the first hundred years after the conquest tell of many trials for this crime. These rustic rituals lacked the pomp which might have lessened their horror in pagan days: they were now mere murders hastily and awkwardly carried out in deserted country churches, or caves, or the bush. The victims were no longer acquiescent, and the priest's promises that the victim would go straight to heaven were now less readily believed. In a pathetic and disgusting attempt to capture the 'power' of the new religion, the clownish and ignorant pagan priests of the villages would, in some cases, crucify their victims. (In some cases the victim would be given, half-contemptuously, the ceremonial name of Jesus Christ.) The noble and exalted elements of the native religion, already debased by centuries of strife, had disappeared. In their place was a clandestine cult which had much in common with the then flourishing witch-cult of Europe, and which, indeed, absorbed elements of European 'underground' beliefs, brought over by the white settlers and conquerors.

'In Pinola', says Gage, 'there were some who were much given to witchcraft, and by the power of the Devil did act strange things.' There was one old woman, Marta de Carrillo, who was suspected by many of being a witch, but when she was brought before the justice she was acquitted since he could find no sure evidence against her. This acquittal emboldened her to practice her arts even more openly: two or three died in Pinola as a result of her machinations. As Gage describes it, they literally withered away, declaring on their deathbeds that Carrillo had killed them, and that they had seen her spirit near their beds, threatening them, and wearing an angry and frowning expression. It was known to be her spirit, since none of the others standing around the beds had seen her.

The Indians were so afraid of her that they did not dare to lay a charge. So Gage himself warned the lord of Pinola, Don Juan de Guzmán, that if her actions were not looked into, she would destroy the town. Guzmán, upon receiving this warning, obtained a commission from the Bishop and another officer of the Inquisition which empowered Gage to make a careful and secret inquiry into her life and actions.

He found that many of the Indians had complaints against her. Most of the town affirmed that she was a notorious witch. It was said that, before she had been brought before the justice, her familiar had been a duck. This duck had followed her wherever she went about the town; it even followed her to church, waiting for her outside the door until she came out. This duck, they said, must have been her devil and familiar spirit, since, when she had it with her, and they set dogs on her, the dogs would not chase her, but ran away. After she had been brought before the justice, though, the duck was not seen with her any more. She had warned her familiar off, it was said, to avoid suspicion.

Though Marta de Carrillo was a widow, and in appearance one of the poorest people of the town, she never seemed to be short of money. During Lent, all the town came to confession, each person bringing his gift. The usual gift was one real; but Carrillo brought four reals, not to mention eggs, fish, a little bottle of honey and a live turkey. Gage was not impressed: he reasoned that she had done this to improve the opinion he had of her.

In her confession she spoke of nothing but trifles, none of which could be called sinful actions. Gage questioned her very closely on the matter of witchcraft, and especially about those who had, in dying, seen her about their beds, threatening them. She replied, weeping, that she was wronged.

How was it, Gage asked her, that she, with no sons to help her, and no apparent means of livelihood, had so much money that she could give more at confession than the richest of the town? How had she come by the turkey and honey, since she kept neither fowls nor bees? God loved her, she said, and had given all those things: the rest, she said, she had bought with her money. When Gage asked who she had bought them from, she said simply that she had bought them in the town.

Gage's answer to this was to urge her to repent, and to reject the devil and all his works; but she only answered like 'a saintly and holy woman', and begged him to give her the Communion with the rest the next day. I dare not do this, Gage answered, and he quoted her the texts about not giving the children's bread unto dogs, and casting one's pearls before the swine; it would be a great scandal, he said, to give the Communion to one generally suspected of being a witch. The old woman began to weep, saying that she had received the Communion for many years, but Gage, unmoved, was resolute in his refusal. He dismissed her, and she left in tears.

At noon, his work in the church done, Gage sent his servant to gather up the offerings. In particular, he was to have Marta de Carrillo's fish dressed for dinner. But when the cook opened the fish in the kitchen, it was full of maggots, and stinking. When Gage was told of this, he opened her gift of honey and poured it into a dish. It was full of worms. Since there had been nearly a hundred eggs offered that day, he could not identify hers; but, out of the eggs he used during the rest of that day, some were rotten, and some had half-formed chicks within them. The next morning, the turkey was found dead. As for her four reals, when he counted the money which had been given him that day, and of which he had kept (who can doubt him?) a careful mental record, he found them missing.

That night the clerk of the church came to Gage, begging him to give Communion to Carrillo, since he feared that, if he did not, some harm would come to him. But Gage refused again.

After his servants had gone to bed, Gage sat up late with his books, preparing his Communion exhortation for the next day. It was between ten and eleven o'clock; he was in his chamber on the ground floor. He heard the hall door fly open; somebody came in, and walked about. Then another door opened, and the foot-steps continued into a little room where the saddles were. Gage thought it might be his friend, the middle-aged 'Blackamoor', Miguel Dalva. Dalva had given him much help in the town; they were on very easy terms, and Dalva often stayed at his house. He called him by name, two or three times, but no answer came. Suddenly another door—it led into the garden—flew open. Gage was now very frightened; his hair, he tells us, was standing on end. He tried to call to his servants, but his voice stuck in his throat. Then, remembering the witch, he put his trust in

God; a degree of self-possession returned to him, along with his voice; and he began to call to his servants, and to bang on the door with his stick, since he was afraid to open it.

The noise woke his servants, and when they came to his door, he summoned up enough courage to open it. Had they heard somebody in the hall, he asked them? Had they heard the doors being opened? They told him they had all been asleep; they had heard nothing. One boy, however, said he had been awake, and had heard just what Gage had heard. Gage picked up his candle, and went into the hall. All the doors were shut, and the servants swore that was just how they had left them. Then Gage perceived that the witch had tried to frighten him, but could do him no harm. He commanded two of his servants to remain in his chamber with him, and went to bed.

Early the next morning he sent for the clerk of the church, and told him what had happened during the night. The clerk smiled. It was the widow Carrillo, doubtless: she had often played such tricks with those in the town who had offended her. After the Communion service that morning, some of the leading Indians of the town came to Gage, and warned him that Carrillo had sworn to do him some mischief or other because he would not give her the sacraments.

Faced with such evidence, Gage could doubt no longer. He sent old Carrillo to the City of Guatemala, with a number of witnesses, and all the evidence which he had found against her (not much, it seems). The President and Bishop commanded her to be put into prison, and there she died within two months.

Even stranger was the case of Juan Gómez. Gómez was the chief of the principal tribe of Pinola and the countryside surrounding it. He was nearly eighty, and was a sort of village oracle, whose advice was sought on all occasions.

Gage had always thought of him as a devout Christian; he never missed morning and evening prayers, and had given the church a good deal of money.

Very suddenly he was taken sick, and the mayordomo of the sodality of the Virgin sent for Gage at Mixco, asking him to come and hear Gómez' confession: Gómez wanted much to see him, and to be comforted by him in his hour of death. Though it was pitch-dark and raining hard, Gage set out to ride the nine miles to his house.

When he arrived at Gómez' house, wet to the skin, he went to the old man's bedside. Gómez' face was heavily bandaged, but through the wrappings he thanked Gage for his charity and the pains he had taken; he confessed his sins with tears, and in his whole manner showed only a Christian character, and a willing desire to die and be with Christ. Gage comforted him and prepared him for death, asking him finally how he felt. The old man replied that he was sick of old age and weakness. With this, Gage went to his house, and laid down to rest. Before he went to sleep, more Indians came to see him: Gómez was about to die, and desired extreme unction. Gage went once again to his house to perform this last rite for the living, and first rite for the dead. He anointed him on the nose, lips, eyes, hands and feet. As he did so, he saw that Gómez' flesh was swollen and discoloured; but he did not think of it, at that time, as coming from anything other than the sickness of his body. It was now daybreak, and he returned home. After he had slept for a while, more Indians came to his door to buy candles to offer up for Gómez' soul: he had died, they said, and was to be buried that day. Groggily, Gage went to the church, and in the churchyard he saw a grave being dug.

Near the church he met two or three Spaniards, who had come into Mass that morning. He began talking about Juan

Gómez. He told them what comfort he himself had received from Gómez' Christian confidence, and that he was sure he would be saved for his godly life, and, finally, that the town would be lessened by his going, since he was the chief guide and leader of the people, full of wisdom and good counsel. The Spaniards smiled at one another. You are much deceived, they said, if you think Gómez was a saint and a holy man. Gage grew somewhat warm at this. You are enemies of the Indians, he said, and you judge them without charity, but I, who know them well from their confessions, can judge them better. It seems, one of them said, that Gómez' confession has told you little about him; apparently you are ignorant of what they say in the town about the real cause of his death. This seemed so strange to Gage that he asked them to explain themselves.

The report was, they said, that Juan Gómez was the chief of the wizards and witches of the town. He commonly took the shape of a puma, or mountain lion, and as such would walk about the mountains. There was one Sebastián López, another old Indian and head of another tribe, who was Gómez' deadly enemy. Two days before Gómez' death, they had met on the mountain—Gómez in the shape of a puma and López in the shape of a jaguar—and there they had fought. Gómez, who was older and weaker, had been much bruised and bitten, and his death had been caused by his wounds. López was now in prison on the charge, and the two tribes were contending: the people of Gómez were demanding compensation from those of López, and threatening to make the matter known to the Spaniards if they were not satisfied. But they were unwilling to do this, preferring to agree and smother it up among themselves, that they might not bring discredit on the whole town.

Gage did not know what to believe now: could Gómez

have deceived him, even on his death-bed? He confirmed that López was in prison by going there himself. He also found out that the town officers, and the chiefs of the tribes concerned, had been considering the matter in the town-house all that morning. Then he called one of the officers of the town, a friend of his, to his house, and questioned him closely. At first the man was reluctant to speak, fearing the whole town would turn against him if he told the truth; but when Gage comforted him with promises that this would not happen, he consented to tell what had occurred.

The story he told was substantially the same as that Gage had heard from the Spaniards. Some of Gómez' friends, he said, would not care if his use of black magic and his dark religious hypocrisy should be known to the world; others, he said, who were as wicked as the two old enemies themselves, wanted the matter kept secret, lest they and all the witches and wizards of the town should be discovered. Gage tells us that this struck him to the very heart. Was it possible that the best people among the Indians, who spent all they could get by their labour upon the church and the saints, should be in league with the devil?

When he had dismissed the Indian, he went to the church, to see if the people were coming to Mass; but he only found two men preparing Gómez' grave. He went back home, much troubled within himself as to whether he should give Gómez a Christian burial. On consideration, he decided he should, since he had only the evidence of the one Indian and the Spaniards, who spoke from hearsay.

At this point, though, a deputation, made up of nearly all the town officials, came to his door. Juan Gómez must not be buried that day, they said; they had decided to call officers of the crown to view his corpse, and examine into the mode of his death, lest questions should rise afterwards, and they

Spaniards taking over Indian lands

Indians at work on the land and in the *obrajes*

Panama in the late seventeenth century

should have to exhume the body. Gage, pretending that he had heard nothing about Gómez, asked them why they wished to do this. They told him then that there were those in the town who had seen a puma and a jaguar fighting, and had presently lost sight of them, and that about the same time they had seen Gómez and López parting from each other. Gómez, covered with bruises, had immediately gone home to his bed, and had never risen again. He had declared on his death-bed that López had killed him, and for this reason they had put López in custody.

They begged Gage not to judge the whole town by these two wicked men, who had constant dealings with the devil, and that they were resolved to root out all such among them. Gage said that he did not think ill of such a laudable endeavour.

That night when the officer of the crown came, and he and Gage together examined Gómez' body, they found it bruised and scratched and bitten in many places. Thus, though a grave had been prepared for him in consecrated ground, he was not buried there, but in a common ditch.

Later López, who made little effort to deny the charges against him, was hanged in the city of Guatemala.

This was Gage's first encounter, though he was not fully aware of the deeper implications of the event, with the *nahualistas*. Like the Leopard-Men of Africa, they were members of a criminal secret society. They followed a perverted and ancient animal cult much older than the official religions of the Aztecs and Toltecs. They identified themselves with the jaguar, with whom, by means of revolting spells and rituals, they tried to establish a kinship. We should not be too quick to laugh at Gage and his villagers. Certainly the two old wizards could not, physically, have changed into jungle cats; but witchcraft is not, after all, concerned with the changing of physical objects. Travellers in Africa have reported seeing strange things which seem to indicate that it is possible for unscrupulous human beings possessing notable spiritual power to identify themselves in some way with animals, and, in a sense 'enter into' their wills.

It is the modern practice, among writers who preserve an open mind on questions of the supernatural, to recount what they have seen, without attempting to explain it. (Indeed, outside the writings of Swedenborg, there is no adequate theory of such phenomena.) If Gage does not confess the bafflement found in modern stories, this is because the theology of his day afforded an explanation of such phenomena as the result of a pact with Satan.

XVIII—*Breaking an Idol*

IN Mixco there were four brothers named Fuentes, who were among the wealthiest and most important of the town. They were very pious in their conversation; they were devoted to the saints, and scrupulously observed all the feast days; yet in private they were idolaters, continuing to worship their gods in the forests and caves around the town. It so happened that one day these, and others of their party, also rich men, were drinking *chicha* in the presence of some Christians. When they were drunk, they fell to boasting of their god, saying that he preached better to them than Gage did, and that he had told them to believe nothing that Gage preached to them of Christ, but to follow their forefathers, who knew how to worship the gods. The Christians were now very curious as to where that idol might be hidden. By pretending to yield to the Fuentes' persuasion to join them

146

in the 'old' worship, they managed to extract this information from them. When they were sober they thought better of it, and agreed to forget what they had heard, but could not forget it so far as to refrain from gossiping about it. Thus the news came to the ears of a Spaniard in the valley, who brought it to Gage.

Gage sent for the Indian from whom the Spaniard had heard the news. The Indian confessed that he had heard of such a thing, but that he was afraid to talk of it, fearing that if he did reveal where the idol was, the Indians would, by the power of their compact with the forces of hell, do him much harm. If you are a true Christian, Gage said, you would fight against the devil fearlessly, knowing that hell cannot harm you if you are with God, and have faith in Christ. Indeed, he added, the discovery of the idol will be a means of converting the idolaters, when they see what little power their false god has against the true God of the Christians.

Furthermore, Gage said, if the Indian did not tell him who the idolatrous Indians were, and where their idol was, he would have him sent to the City of Guatemala, where the justices would force the facts out of him.

At this, the Indian agreed to tell all he knew. The Fuentes, he said, had talked of a cave in a certain mountain, with a spring and a pine tree at its mouth. He could not be more specific: he had often been in that mountain, where he had seen two or three springs of water, but he had never been in any cave. Will you come with me, said Gage, to discover the cave? The Indian refused. He tried to persuade Gage not to go, lest, if the idolaters should be in their cave, they should kill them rather than allow themselves to be discovered. I will go with a guard, Gage said, and as to their false god, it has no power to hurt a Christian.

Gage decided to take with him the Indian, the Spaniard who had first told him of the idolaters, three or four additional Spaniards, and his mulatto friend, Miguel Dalva. He would not let the Indian return to his house, for fear he should reveal Gage's purpose in the town, thus forewarning the Fuentes to remove their idol. The Indian still refused to accompany him, and once more Gage threatened to send for the officers of justice. The Indian gave in, and Gage dismissed him in the custody of the Spanish informant, who was to keep close watch and guard over him until they met the next day.

That day he rode to Pinola and summoned Miguel Dalva, but without telling him why he wanted him back in Mixco. He also went to four Spaniards, his neighbours, and told them to be ready the next morning to go a little way with him 'for the service of God'. They should bring their fowling pieces, in case they should 'find some sport', and Gage would be responsible for the wine and meat. They readily agreed, thinking that, though he had talked of the service of God, he was simply inviting them to go on a hunting party. Gage was quite content that they should think that way. He went home, and had his servant prepare a good gammon of bacon, and some roasted and boiled fowls.

The next morning the party travelled towards the area in which the idolaters celebrated their clandestine rites. This was in a wood some six miles from Mixco, towards the town of San Juan Sacatepéquez. Shortly after they entered the wood, they came upon a deep *barranca*, or glen, with a stream running at its bottom. It seemed a likely place, but though they searched diligently, they could find nothing. (We must assume that by now every member of the party knew what they were hunting.)

They climbed up the side of the *barranca*, and, after careful investigation, found a spring of water, but no cave. Evening was now coming on, and some of the party began to speak of returning home; but Gage thought it best to stay there the night. If they returned home without success, he reasoned, the idolaters might well suspect the purpose for which they had been out. It would then be easy for them to rush to their secret place and remove the idol. The company accepted his reasoning, and they decided to stay in the *barranca* for the night. When they had made a fire, they had a supper of cold meat and hot chocolate.

In the morning they prayed for guidance, that they might discover 'the cave of darkness and iniquity where lay hid that instrument of Satan'. They entered the thick wood on the side of a steep hill, and searched its south and north sides without success.

Then, as they were descending the north side, they found a poorly marked path, which they followed until they came to another spring of water. When they had searched carefully about it, they found some pieces of broken earthenware, and a piece of a chafing dish, such as the Indians used to burn copal (Gage calls it 'frankincense') before the images of the saints. It did not seem unlikely to the searchers that they would use similar dishes to burn incense before their idols. Further, they could identify the pottery as having come from Mixco. Almost immediately, they found the pine tree which the Indian had described to them. Near-by was the cave. It was very dark within, but light at the mouth, and near the mouth they found earthenware dishes, with ashes in them —the remains of some copal incense. They struck fire, lit a couple of candles, and went in.

At the entrance the cave was broad, and penetrated into the mountain in a straight line; then it turned towards the left. When they had followed this branch some eleven yards, they found the idol. It was standing on a low stool, which was covered with a linen cloth. Though it was made of wood, it was black and shiny, as if it had been painted or smoked, and it was in the form of a man's head and shoulders. The idol had neither beard nor moustache; his expression was grim, his forehead was wrinkled, and his eyes were big and startled. However, 'we feared not his frowning look', says Gage. They lifted up the idol, and underneath they found a few reals, left there by the worshippers. On the ground about the image they found other simple offerings—single reals, a few plantains and other fruits, little jars of maize and honey, some half-burned candles, and little dishes on which incense had been burned.

These were precisely the things which were regularly given to the saints in Gage's church, some of which, he remarks dryly, were no handsomer than this idol. (Indeed, when Gage questioned the idolaters later, he expected them to say that it was the image of a saint, and thus to excuse themselves; but they did not; he was their god, they said, who had spoken and preached to them, and he was above all the saints in the country.)

The party now began to cut down the boughs of trees; they filled the cave with them, and stopped up its mouth. Then they came away, having wrapped the idol in cloth, and given it to the Indian to carry on his back. Gage thought it best to wait till nightfall before they entered Mixco, so that the idolaters might suspect nothing. He stayed at the house of one of the Spaniards until nightfall, and before he left asked him to warn all the Spaniards in that area to be at Mixco Church the next Sunday, because he had something to say to them and their negro slaves concerning their sodalities. He wanted the Spaniards there in case the idolaters— he did not know how many there were—should rise up against them; but he could not tell them why they were needed, for fear the idolaters, hearing of it, would stay away. Miguel Dalva, who was anxious to see the end of the business, stayed with him, and accompanied him home.

On the Sunday morning, before the service, he had Miguel Dalva carry the idol, still wrapped in its cloth, into the church, and hide it in the pulpit. Then he set Dalva to watch the church till the congregation came in, that none might see it, or take it away. He further commanded Dalva to be near the pulpit at sermon time, and to warn some negro friends of his, and those Spaniards who were aware of what was going on, to post themselves unobtrusively near the pulpit stairs.

That day the church was as full as Gage had wished it to be. The Spaniards were there, and the negroes, and among the Indians were the Fuentes and the other suspected idolaters, all quite ignorant of what Gage had in mind.

The Mass having been celebrated, Gage entered the pulpit for the sermon. He had chosen as his text the third verse of the twentieth chapter of *Exodus*—'Thou shalt have none other gods before me,' though in fact it was not the text of the day in the Roman calendar. The congregation looked at each other: they were not used to hearing sermons based on Old Testament texts. Gage then expanded on his text, his intention being to show that no finite creature could have the power of God the Creator, nor could any man do good or evil without His will or permission. If this was true of men, how much more was it true of inanimate creatures, such as idols.

The sermon half finished, he bent down in the pulpit, lifted up 'the black, grim and staring devil', and placed it on one side of the pulpit. He looked upon the Fuentes, and some of the others, and he saw that they changed colour, and looked at each other. Gage asked the congregation to see the god that some of them worshipped, and to ask themselves if they knew whence he had come, or what part of the earth he ruled. Some had boasted, he said, that that piece of wood had spoken and preached against Christ, and therefore they worshipped it as a god, and offered it honey, fruit and coins, and burned incense before it in a hidden place. Did they not show by this that they were ashamed to acknowledge him publicly, and did not his lurking in the darkness of the earth show plainly that he belonged to the Prince of Darkness?

Now Gage challenged the idol to speak for itself, or else by its silence to show it had no power. He taunted it, defying Satan, who had used it as an instrument, and daring the Devil to take it from the pulpit, if he could. Then he said to the Indians that if their god had power to deliver him from the execution he intended, which was to cut him in pieces and burn him, they should not believe the Gospel of Jesus Christ; but if the god had no power against him, the weakest instrument of the true and living God, then they should forsake their folly, and embrace Christ. He further promised them that, if they should renounce their superstitious worship, he would protect them from all punishments.

When he had concluded, he came down from the pulpit, and commanded the idol to be brought down after him. He sent out for an axe and two or three great pans of coals, and then he commanded that the idol be cut into very small pieces, and thrown on the burning coals; this was done, and the idol was burned before the congregation. At this the Spaniards cried out joyfully, *Victor, victor!* and *Gloria a nuestro Dios!*; but the idolaters did not speak a word. And with that the service ended.

Later Gage wrote the President of Guatemala, informing

him of what he had done. He also wrote the Bishop, asking him what should be done further, since he did not know how deep the rot of idolatry ran in the town. The reply from both was that he should discover as many of the idolaters as he could, and endeavour to convert them by fair and gentle means, to show pity on their blindness, and to promise them that on repentance they would be pardoned by the Inquisition, 'which, considering them to be but new plants, useth not such rigour with them which it useth with Spaniards if they fall into such horrible sins'.

Gage followed this advice. He asked the Fuentes to come to him privately. He told them how merciful the Inquisition was to them, expecting their conversion and amendment. But their demeanour was stubborn and angry, for, they said, not only they, but many others in that town and in the town of San Juan Sacatépequez, worshipped that same god. It is only a piece of wood, Gage said, so how can it be a god? We know it is only a piece of wood, one of them replied, and we know it cannot speak of itself; but we have all heard it speak. We believe God is in that wood, because if it speaks it must be something extraordinary. Certainly, it deserves more adoration than those saints in the church, who never speak to the people.

If you have heard it speak, Gage said, then it spoke of the Devil, not of God, because it preached against Christ, the only begotten Son of God. But they only answered that their forefathers had never known who Christ was until the Spaniards came into their country, but they had known there were gods, and they had worshipped them and sacrificed to them. For all they knew, they said, this god might have belonged to their forefathers.

Gage, seeing that he could not reason with them, told them to leave him.

153

From now on, Gage went in danger of his life. Twice the Fuentes, or some accomplices, entered his house and tried to get into his chamber. But the first time he awoke his servants, and they fled; and the second time, they were driven out by Miguel Dalva, who was now staying with Gage as a bodyguard. Yet they were always courteous when they encountered Gage in the street.

Then, almost three months after the burning of the idol, there came a messenger to say that Pablo, the oldest of the Fuentes, was dying, and that he wished Gage to convert him to the true religion. Gage was made very happy by this; he prayed that God would help him plead His cause, and he at once set out for Pablo's house.

When he had come to the door, and had entered one step, he found three of the Fuentes brothers, and some suspected idolaters, sitting about the room. Pablo was not there. Gage nervously withdrew his foot a little, and asked where Pablo was. They stood up and looked at him, but said no word. Gage, suspecting some treachery, turned about to leave, just in time to catch Pablo, the supposed invalid, creeping up on him with a cudgel in his hand, which he had lifted for the blow. Gage caught the stick with both hands as it came down, and while they were struggling with the stick, the Indians in the house ran into the yard and beset Gage, pulling him here and there and tearing his clothes. One ran his knife into Gage's hand to make him drop the stick (the scar remained with him all his life); but, because it was a public place, he did not dare to stab him in any vital part. When they saw he would not let go of the cudgel, another of the Fuentes took hold of it with Pablo, and they thrust it against his mouth with such force that they broke some of his teeth and his mouth filled with blood.

With this blow he was knocked down, but he soon re-

covered, and rose. They stood by, laughing at him, but did
not dare to do him any more harm, for fear they should be
seen. Indeed, they had already been seen. A mulatto slave
girl was passing by, and heard Gage's cry for help—a hope-
less cry, as it seemed, since all the houses in that neighbour-
hood belonged to the Fuentes. Seeing Gage covered in blood,
she thought he had been mortally wounded, and ran off
along the street, crying; 'Murder, murder in Pablo Fuentes
his yard!' In the market-place and town-house she found the
mayor and the officers of justice, who all came running, and
with them two Spaniards with drawn swords.

Now Gage had to protect his assailant. The other attackers
had run away, but he had held tight to Pablo. The Spaniards
made to kill him on the spot; but Gage forbade this. Pablo
Fuentes was taken off to prison.

That night the other idolaters and conspirators were taken,
and also confined to prison. Later, they were brought to trial.
They were whipped through the streets, and two of them
were banished far away from their native town. All of them
would have been banished, had they not pleaded with Gage
to get them off, with promises to amend their lives. They
confessed that the Devil had greatly tempted them, and that
now they were prepared to forsake all their idolatries, and
live thereafter as good Christians. Gage, much moved by
their fears, interceded for them. Thereafter, he said, for as
long as he lived in that town, he found a great change in
their lives, which gave him every reason to believe their
repentance was unfeigned.

Since we have evidence that Gage was capable of shameful
and perfidious behaviour, let this good deed be recorded in
his favour. He was genuinely concerned with the Indians'
spiritual welfare; indeed, he loved them, and thought them
'of a good and flexible nature'. Part of his hatred of Roman

Catholicism, which caused him later to commit acts which seem unforgivable, must have received its final crystallization at Mixco. It was at Mixco he realized that the Mexican Church was Janus-faced. It had introduced Christianity; but it had also substituted the worship of the saints for that of the gods. In many cases, this had only involved the worshipping of idols with new names, depicted in a different art style, and representative of a different mystical cosmology.

XIX—*Gage Runs Away Again*

THE year was 1635. In this year, Gage received the letter he had been waiting for: he learned that the General of the Dominican Order in Rome had given him a licence to return to England. He was, indeed, weary of the New World: he had had little success in his efforts to help the Indians to advance beyond the merely formal Christianity they professed. Also, the Spaniard who was lord of the town of Mixco, a man little concerned with orthodoxy, was offended with him for having caused two of his town to be banished, and having caused an uproar over the affair of the idol. Accordingly, Gage wrote to his Provincial, who was then in Chiapa, asking for permission to return home. But the Provincial was now Jacinto de Cabañas, the very man who had sponsored, when he was Prior of the Guatemala cloister, Gage's debate with the Jesuits. Now he was more than ever convinced of Gage's value. Unwilling to lose so devoted a priest as Gage had shown himself to be (a priest, moreover, who spoke Pokoman) he appointed him vicar of the town of Amatitlán.

After a year, Gage tried again. By this time, Rev. Fr.

Jacinto de Cabañas had been replaced by Rev. Fr. Pedro de Montenegro, who simply transferred him from Amatitlán to the town of Petapa, where he stayed another year.

Finally, seeing that his superiors would never let him go, Gage decided to run away.

He could not afford to confide his plans to anybody: even his best friend might betray him. Yet it would have been a hard thing to run away alone, without some friend near him for the first two or three days' journey. There was another matter to be considered also: he had many things to sell, and he needed somebody to do this for him. He could think of no man better able to help him in this than Miguel Dalva, whom he knew, from long experience, to be honest and trustworthy. He sent for him, and, swearing him to secrecy, told him that he had to make a journey to Rome for his conscience' sake. He did not tell him the truth, that he was going to England, for fear that 'the good old Blackamoor' would, for the love he bore Gage, seek to prevent a journey from which his friend would never return. He would not be so alarmed by a trip to Rome: many, after all, had taken the same journey, and returned within two years.

Dalva wanted to go with Gage to Rome, but Gage refused, saying that the sea-journey would be too hard on a man of his age, and, furthermore, that as a free blackamoor in Europe, he might at any time be arrested on suspicion of being an escaped slave. Dalva could hardly fail to see the logic in this. Finally he asked only that he be allowed to accompany Gage to the seashore.

When Gage had sold his pictures, books and household furnishings, and had added to this the sum he had amassed during his twelve years in the New World, he found that he had nine thousand pieces of eight. There were no bank-notes or travellers' cheques in those days, and this was too heavy a load of wealth for a long journey. So he converted about four thousand crowns into pearls and precious stones, and the rest of the coins he laid up in bags or sewed into his quilt. Then he laid in some food for the journey.

He knew he would have to travel fast the first week. So he sent his chest on ahead of him, in the care of an Indian from Mixco whom he trusted well. Four days later he himself left, accompanied only by Miguel Dalva. He left when all the Indians were asleep, leaving nothing in his lodgings but old papers, and the key in the door. In this manner, Gage bade farewell to Guatemala.

He was fleeing towards Granada, on Lake Nicaragua. He had examined the other possibilities and rejected them. The ports on the Gulf of Honduras were the closest; but he knew that there he would, in all probability, meet people he knew. In any case, the ships left there so infrequently that orders to stop his escape might well arrive from Guatemala before he had embarked. To go through Mexico to Vera Cruz would be even more dangerous.

He left the week after Christmas, knowing that the ships commonly left Granada for Havana after the middle of January. He also had Miguel Dalva send a letter to a friend of his, which was in turn to be posted to the Provincial in Guatemala four days after his departure. In this letter he took his leave of the Provincial, asking him not to blame him or seek after him, since he had a licence from Rome to leave. And in order that the Provincial might not look for him in Nicaragua, he dated and subscribed the letter from the town of San Antonio Suchitepéquez, which was on the way to Mexico.

Until he reached the Rio Lempa, he was very careful not to travel through any large Spanish town, particularly one in which there might be a Dominican cloister. But when he reached this river, 'some ten leagues from San Salvador', he was able to relax, since

'This river is privileged in this manner, that if a man commit any heinous crime or murder on this side of Guatemala, and San Salvador, or on the other side of St Miguel or Nicaragua, if he can flee to get over this river, he is free as long as he liveth on the other side, and no justice on that side whither he is escaped can question or trouble him for the murder committed. So likewise for debts he cannot be arrested. Though I thanked God I neither fled for the one, or for the other, yet it was my comfort that I was now going over to a privileged country, where I hoped I would be free and sure . . .

'We ferried safely over the river; and from thence went in company with my Indian to a small town of Indians two leagues off, where we made the best dinner that we had done from the town of Petapa, and willingly gave rest to all our mules till four of the clock in the afternoon.'

From the Rio Lempa he travelled to Realejo, and 'from hence to Granada I observed nothing but the plainness and pleasantness of the way, which with the fruits and fertility of all things may well make Nicaragua the Paradise of America'. Thus Gage arrived safely at Granada on the lake, having caught up with his chest on the way. He was happy enough when he got there, thinking that he had no more land journeys to make until he should land at Dover in England, and post up to London. It was time to think of dismissing Dalva and the Indian; but Dalva refused to leave him until he had seen him safely aboard ship. The Indian was also willing to stay, but Gage would not allow this, knowing he had a wife and children at home. The Indian then declared himself perfectly willing to return home on foot, offering to let Gage sell the mules to make what money he could of them; but Gage, touched by this kindness, insisted that he accept enough money to cover his expenses home, and to keep himself for a while after he arrived. The Indian wept when he said goodbye, the third day after they arrived in Granada, saying that he would never see Gage again.

Gage and Dalva, left alone, discovered that the frigates would not be departing for a fortnight, so they decided to spend a day or two looking at 'that stately and pleasant tówn'. After that, they would take refuge in some nearby Indian town until the frigate sailed; for at that time many mule-trains were arriving from Guatemala, laden with indigo and cochineal for shipment to Spain, and there was always the possibility that somebody in the train might recognize them. Though Granada was on Lake Nicaragua, it was in effect a sea-port, since the ships passed from the lake to the sea by the San Juan River, or the Desaguadero ('channel'), as it was then called.

Granada they found to be a moneyed town, in which were some very wealthy merchants and a number of prosperous if less wealthy ones, most of whom traded along the Caribbean coast of Central and South America.

Its wealth was greatly increased while they were there. The Gulf of Honduras was infested, at that time, by the ships of Dutch pirates, and for this reason the merchants of Guatemala were sending their goods to Granada, that they might be shipped to Cartagena in what is now Colombia, and thence to Spain.

The town they chose to go to was a league from Granada; and here Gage was frequently entertained by the Mercedarian Friars, the most powerful order in the Indian towns of Nicaragua. Here also he made some inquiries about the journey to Cartagena. The answers he received were discouraging. Ships could cross the lake with ease, but the hundred mile journey down the Rio Desaguadero to the sea, was quite another matter. Sometimes the river voyage lasted

two months: because of the rapids, they had to unload the
boats many times, and then load them again when the dangerous water had been passed. (The cargo was stored in a
series of warehouses along the bank, while the boat, lightened
of its load, passed through the rapids.) The gnats were intolerable, and passengers had been known to die of the heat
before they reached the sea. It was distressing news indeed;
yet he comforted himself that few frigates had been lost on the
river, and that his life was, after all, in the hands of God.

Every so often Gage would go to Granada, to find out
when the frigates were leaving, and to bargain for his
passage. He found a captain, and settled with him for a place
at his table. But, when they were within four or five days of
departure, frustrating news arrived from Guatemala: it was
ordered that the frigates should not go out that year. Apparently some English or Dutch ships were lying in wait off
the mouth of the Rio Desaguadero. News like this was
frightening not only to the merchants, understandably fearful
of losing a fortune to the pirates, but to the President himself,
who was responsible for the King's revenues, and would be
held to account if, rashly ignoring due warning, he allowed
them to depart on a ship which stood a good chance of being
captured.

This left Gage at loose ends. He thought of the ship which
ran between Realejo and Panama, but discovered that it had
already set sail, as had the small ships from the ports of
Honduras. Other passengers for Spain were in the same
position; and when Gage consulted with them, they thought
of hiring a frigate to carry them to Cartagena, but could not
find a master willing to risk his ship at such a dangerous
time.

Thus Gage haunted the quays of Granada, his hopes
fading. At last he met a merchant, who gave him some

advice. Gage should go, he said, to the port of Cartago in Costa Rica. There he would be sure to find a small coastal vessel bound for Portobello, laden with meal, bacons, fowls, and other provisions for the galleons. It was a long chance, and the journey to Cartago would not be at all pleasant: he would have to travel almost a hundred and fifty leagues, over mountains and through deserts, and he might, in the end, not encounter a ship. But anything seemed preferable to returning to Guatemala; even the long doubtful journey, and the waiting in Portobello till June or July, the months in which the galleons left for Spain. To three Spaniards he had encountered, the risk seemed worthwhile, and the four agreed to set out on the journey together.

Dalva would gladly have gone with him: indeed, he would have gone around the world with Gage, but this the latter would not permit. He thanked Dalva for what he had done, gave him money for the trip home, and dismissed him. The four companions set out from Granada on muleback, following the shore of the lake of Nicaragua.

On the second day out of the town, Gage had an adventure, which he records thus—

'The second day after we set out we were much affrighted with a huge and monstrous cayman or crocodile, which, having come out of the lake (which we passed by), and lying across a puddle of water bathing himself, and waiting for some prey, as we perceived after, when we, not knowing well at the first, but thinking that it had been some tree that was felled or fallen, passed close by it; when on a sudden we knew the scales of the cayman, and saw the monster stir and move, and set himself against us; wherewith we made haste from him, but he thinking to have made some of us his greedy prey, ran after us, which when we perceived, and that he was like to overtake us, we were much troubled, until one of the Spaniards (who knew better the nature and quality of that beast than the rest) called upon us to turn to one side out of the way, and to ride on straight for a while, and then to turn to another side, and so to circumflex our way, which advice without doubt saved mine or some of the others' lives, for thus we wearied that mighty monster and escaped from him, who had we rid our straight way, had certainly overtaken us and killed some mule or man, for his straightforward flight was as swift as our mules could run—'

Was Gage's monster an alligator, a cayman, or that much rarer beast, the *Crocodilus americanus*? Crocodiles and alligators can move with some speed on land, and it is certainly true that, since they can only run in a straight line, they may be evaded by a zigzag flight. Perhaps Gage was so frightened, never having encountered such an animal before, that he thought it was moving as fast as his mule.

On the second or third day they left Lake Nicaragua, and began to strike across rough and mountainous country towards the city of Cartago. They had been informed that a frigate would soon be setting out from the mouth of the River Sueré (now called the Pacuaré). After four days' rest in Cartago, they set out again. The country they were travelling through was mountainous, with occasional valleys in which Spaniards and Indians lived on isolated farms, growing a little maize and breeding a few hogs. They arrived at the mouth of the Sueré three days before their ship was to depart.

The master of the frigate was very glad to have them aboard. Indeed, he offered to carry Gage for nothing to Portobello, declaring that he would be content if Gage merely spent his time praying for him and the safety of his ship. Not that the cargo of the ship would be very attractive to pirates: it consisted only of honey, hides, bacon, meat and fowls.

They weighed anchor, and headed towards the open sea. The mouth of the Sueré was rather dangerous: the river ran with a strong current, and the bay was shallow in some places, and crowded with rocks in others, but they reached open water without mishap.

When they had sailed no more than twenty leagues in open sea, they saw two ships making towards them. The passengers were very alarmed, especially since they could see that the captain, who suspected the ships to be English or Dutch, was looking rather worried himself. Their ship was not armed: the only weapons on board were four or five muskets, and half a dozen swords. It was a small, swift craft, which was some comfort; but they had not sailed more than five leagues further when they perceived that the ships were gaining on them, and that they were Hollanders.

Soon one of them, a man-of-war, fetched up, and fired a shot across their bow. They could do nothing but yield, and hope for mercy. 'But O, what sad thoughts did here run to and fro my dejected heart, which was struck down lower than our sail. How did I sometimes look upon death's frightening visage!' Even if Gage escaped death, what would happen to his 'treasure of pearls, precious stones, and pieces of eight, and golden pistoles'?

Gage had little time for Baroque meditations on death and fortune, since the Dutch, bristling with swords, muskets and pistols, boarded them almost immediately. But Gage and the other passengers felt a little better when they learned who the pirate captain was. He was Diego el Mulato, who had some four years earlier sacked Campeche. This was hardly a recommendation; but they knew that Diego had been born and brought up among the Spaniards of Havana. Thus he was preferable to a Dutchman, who could not be expected to show any mercy to Spaniards.

Diego was, as his name indicates, a mulatto. He was a proud man. When some Spaniards in Havana had whipped him for an offence he had not committed, he had stolen a small boat and taken it out to sea. There he had found some Dutch ships lying in wait for a prize, and he had offered himself to them, promising to serve them against his own countrymen.

So well had he done this that the Hollanders had grown to respect him. They had given him a Dutch girl as his wife, and had made him captain of a ship under Pie de Palo, or Wooden Leg, a Dutch captain much feared by the Spaniards.

There was little to seize on the ship—little, that is, except Gage's money, that money which he had amassed over such a long time, and at such peril to his soul. Diego took from him four thousand pieces of eight in pearls and precious stones, and almost three thousand more in coins. From the other Spaniards, he took some hundreds apiece. It was a richer haul than he had expected: as a result he took little interest at first in the cargo of the ship. Nor was he interested in Gage's other belongings. He did leave him his quilt, some books, some holy pictures, and his clothes, 'which I begged of that noble captain the mulatto'.

It is admittedly unusual for the victim to call the robber 'noble'; but in the continual, undeclared war which England was carrying on with Spain, pirates and free-booters had a strange and particular status. At the time he wrote his book, Gage was more concerned with pandering to the fixed ideas of the English public than with defending his own name; he is also perfectly willing to present this mishap as a Providential chastisement of his own greed, the only sin he admits in himself. Diego, who seems to have possessed the shoddy gallantry of the true seventeenth-century pirate, allowed Gage to keep these articles, which had little resale value, as if this were an act of extraordinary generosity. He added that he could hardly do otherwise than take his money and pearls, 'using that common proverb at sea—*Hoy por mi, mañana por ti*—today fortune hath been for me, tomorrow it may be for thee'.

Luckily, in the quilt which Diego el Mulato had so generously allowed him to keep, he had sewed up a few pistoles, and a few more were sewed up in his doublet: the sum came to almost a thousand crowns.

After the captain and soldiers had thoroughly examined the ship, and taken everything of monetary value, they began to think of the provisions it carried. With its cargo, the 'good captain' gave a dinner in his own frigate, to which Gage was invited. Many healths were traded back and forth. Among them, Diego drank one to his mother, asking Gage to see her and remember him to her, and adding that it was for her sake that he had, while taking from them all their goods, done it with such courtesy and good temper. And he added that, for Gage's sake, he would let them keep their ship, so that they might return to land and find some safer way of reaching Portobello.

After dinner, Gage talked alone to Diego. He told him that he was no Spaniard, but an Englishman born; he showed him the licence he had from Rome to go to England, and said he hoped that, since the English were not at that moment at enmity with the Hollanders, the good captain might give back what goods belonged to him. But his pleas made little impression on Diego, who had already taken possession of all the valuable goods in the ship; he said that Gage must suffer along with those among whom he had been found, and that he might as well claim all the goods in the ship as his own. Gage then asked him if he would carry him to Holland, that he might get to England from that country;

but Diego refused this also, saying that he went about from one place to another, and did not know when he would return to Holland. Furthermore, he said, they were ready every day to fight any Spanish ship they encountered; and if Gage should be on board when such an encounter took place, his men might, in hot blood, do him some mischief, thinking he would harm them by his testimony if the Spaniards should take them captive. Gage saw that there was no hope of getting back what he had lost, so he commended himself to God, and decided to be patient.

The rest of that day and part of the next, the Dutch pirates began to unload the cargo of the coastal boat into their man-of-war. They had changed their minds about seizing only 'legitimate' prizes, money and goods with an immediate cash value: they had decided that the fowls and bacon could be eaten as well as their own, that the meal would be useful to make bread, the honey to sweeten their food, and the hides to make them shoes and boots. In the end, they stripped the ship bare, leaving only enough food to satisfy the stomachs of the crew and passengers till they should make land, which was not far off.

'Thus they took their leave of us, thanking us for their good entertainment,' no doubt with all the contemptible flourishes of the pirate, who, like his contemporary the highwayman, or the modern Mafia gangster, adhered to a grotesque perversion of the honour code of the military aristocrat.

When the four travellers had returned to Sueré, the Spaniards of the towns in the area pitied their condition, and took up a collection for them.

The four, aided by this act of charity, made up their minds to return once again to Cartago, and thence to set out for a more practical port. On the way, they compared notes as to what they had saved. The three Spaniards who had accompanied Gage were in a somewhat better state than he was, for though they had lost all their money, and most of their best clothes, they had reserved some bills of exchange for money to be taken up at Portobello. Gage regretted that he did not have his money in bills like these, which had some of the advantages of the modern cheque. He had learned to be close-mouthed, and he did not tell them of the coins he had saved.

When they came to Cartago, they aroused much pity, and another collection was taken up. Gage officiated at Mass, and preached sermons wherever he went, and in this way he began again to accumulate a little money. The travellers agreed among themselves that they would look as poor and miserable as possible, so that the Indians and Spaniards on the way might be more disposed to give them money.

Nevertheless, Gage knew that in such a comparatively poor country, a country in which he was, moreover, un- known, he could not possibly accumulate enough to allow him to land in England with a full purse. For a moment he thought of returning to Guatemala to begin once again the laborious process of raking in money; but it seemed better to him that he should go home, even if he had to beg his bread on the way. He was by now, he tells us, thoroughly disillu- sioned with Roman Catholicism. Yet he continued to preach, fearful that the Spaniards might ask themselves why he re- fused to exercise his orders and function.

At Cartago, he inquired how he might get to Portobello. Once again, the news was discouraging. There were trains of mules which went over the mountains of Veragua to be sold in Panama. This was the only land traffic into that moun- tainous isthmus, and it was extremely dangerous, not only because of the crags, rocks and mountains which had to be crossed, but more specifically because the unconquered

Indians of the region regularly raided these mule-trains—not for plunder, since the mules themselves were travelling un-laden, but out of pure hatred for the Spaniards. Only recently, he had heard, there had been such an attack, in which some Spaniards had been killed.

There was only one alternative, and that was to retrace their steps, to go to Nicoya in Nicaragua, and thence to the Gulf of Salinas, on the Pacific Coast of Nicaragua. Here they would be able to take ship to Panama. There was, after all, less danger that pirates would be waiting outside Panama, which was a Pacific port.

The way from Cartago to Nicoya was mountainous, and the towns and ranches were poor and insignificant. Nicoya itself, the administrative centre of that region, was, however, a pretty little town.

Gage tells a story about Nicoya which once again reveals that conflict between church and colonists on the question of the just treatment of the Indians, a conflict which seems to have been universal in Spanish America. It also shows that, in spite of its venality and money-grubbing, the church did, on occasion, act in accord with the doctrine it professed.

The *Alcalde Mayor* (this title was given to the governor of a city and its surrounding districts) was one Justo de Salazar. He entertained the travellers well, and provided lodgings for them. He also reassured them by saying that, while there were no ships in the Gulf of Salinas at the moment, he was sure that one would come from Panama very soon. It was that time of year when the coastal ships came for salt and other goods.

They had arrived in Lent. This was a good time, it seemed to Gage, in which to make money, because of the increase in the numbers of those who came to town for confession and Communion. He went to see the Franciscan who had 'the pastorship and charge' of the town, and an arrangement was made.

Now this friar had special reasons for desiring the assistance of Gage.

Some three weeks earlier, he had had a quarrel with de Salazar which had almost resulted in his death. The *Alcalde Mayor* was a notable oppressor of the Indians: he employed them in his and his wife's service as if they had been slaves, refusing to pay them their wages, keeping them from their homes and their wives, and commanding them to work for him on Sundays as on any other day. Accordingly, the friar commanded his Indians from the pulpit not to obey such commands, since they were unlawful. But Justo de Salazar was a hot-blooded man, skilled in fighting, and trained in the wars: he could not accept reproof from a mere friar on such matters as his treatment of Indians and his style of money-making. At first the quarrel was only verbal, and many hot words passed between them. But one day, words having ailed him, the *Alcalde Mayor* came to the friar's house with his sword drawn. The friar, who was as courageous as the *Alcalde*, stood against him, thinking that Salazar would not strike him, for fear of excommunication. Salazar was so provoked by this that he did what he had, perhaps, not expected to do: he lifted up his sword and struck at the friar. His first blow struck off two of the friar's fingers. There was no second because the Indians who served the priest pulled him by main force into his chamber, and shut the door on him, in order to protect him from his own courage.

Justo was indeed excommunicated; but since he was a man of wealth and influence, he managed to obtain a release from the excommunication by an appeal to the Bishop of Costa Rica. Not content with this, he malignantly complained to the Council of Guatemala against the friar; and there, using his friends and money, he caused the friar to be brought before the court. The upshot of it was that the friar was condemned to be removed from Nicoya.

The friar had not left when Gage arrived, but kept to his house and chamber, refusing to go to the church to say Mass, preach or hear confessions. He did have one assistant, but one was not enough at that time, since the church was thronged with 'many hundred Indians, Spaniards, Blackamoors and mulattoes', who had come up for Lent. Thus Gage became his second assistant, and for this he was rewarded with board and lodging at the friar's house, a crown a day for saying Mass plus the voluntary offerings of the people, and a fee for each sermon he preached. From the second week of Lent to Easter week, Gage made a hundred and fifty crowns.

The week before Easter, news came that a frigate was on its way from Panama to the Salinas Gulf. Shortly thereafter the master of the frigate came to Nicoya, which was, as we have seen, the chief town of the area. Gage and his three companions hastened to meet him, and made arrangements for their passage to Panama.

They travelled with him to the Salinas Gulf, and boarded the ship, which was laden with the usual commodities of the country—fowls, salt, honey, maize and some wheat. More important than these workaday goods, though, was the chief and richest cargo of the ship, a certain purple dye made by the Indians from the *Purpura* shellfish. This dye had been made, in pre-Columbian times, from the Pacific Coast of Mexico down to Peru: the process, which is complicated, resembles that involved in the manufacture of 'Tyrian purple'.

Once he was on the boat, Gage thought his troubles were over: he would be in Panama in five or six days, and his return home was only a matter of time. But on their first day out of the gulf, a storm arose, which drove them towards the south; after that, another storm drove them back towards the mountains of Veragua, north of Panama. Some said there must surely be an excommunicated person aboard, and that, if they could discover him, they would throw him overboard. They were becalmed, until 'a strong current' took them out to sea again. The water ran out, and they had nothing to drink for four days: Gage was reduced to drinking his own urine, and sucking on bullets. Nevertheless, the captain refused to stop at an island in order to pick up water, assuring them he would have them all safe and sound in Panama in a day. At this, some of the mariners, along with the three Spaniards accompanying Gage, drew their swords, and forced him to put into an island.

On the evening of the next day, they arrived at Puerto de Perico, outside Panama.

XX—*Portobello*

FOR fifteen days, Gage stayed in the Dominican cloister at Panama. He was, as always, very curious about the city; he had the obsessive and indefatigable curiosity of the good travel-writer. He noted that the city was governed, like Guatemala, by a president, six judges and a Court of Chancery, and that it was a bishop's see. It was more strongly fortified towards the Pacific than any other American port on that ocean, and the defences were armed with ordnance. Yet the houses themselves were as flimsy as those of Vera Cruz; lime and stone were hard to come by, and most of them were made of wood. The President's house, even the richest churches, were mere board constructions, covered with tiles. Because of the heat, the common clothing of the inhabitants

172

was 'a linen cut doublet, with some slight stuff or taffeta breeches'. Gage adds, 'The Spaniards are in this city much given to sin, looseness and venery especially, ... [and they] ... make the Blackamoors (who are many, rich and gallant) the chief objects of their lust.'

Panama was thought at this time to be one of the richest places in America, but only in the sense that Vera Cruz was rich, that is, that wealth was in continual passage through it. Goods from the Atlantic trade came overland or via the River Chagres (which would, much later, become part of the Panama Canal system). Over the Pacific, Panama traded with Peru, the East Indies, and the western ports of Mexico and Central America. For all that, it was a small town, with some five thousand inhabitants, and eight cloisters of nuns and friars.

Gage, fearful of disease in a town noted for its high mortality rate, left Panama as soon as he could. One could travel to Portobello either by land or by water. But the mountains made travel difficult, and for this reason he decided to go by the River Chagres. He set out at midnight for Venta de Cruces, some thirty to thirty-five miles from Panama.

Having travelled by night to avoid the heat, he and his companions arrived, by ten the next morning, at Venta de Cruces, 'where live none but mulattoes and blackamoors, who belong unto the flat boats that carry the merchandise to Portobello'. Gage was well received by these people, who asked him to preach to them the following Sunday, and gave him twenty crowns for a sermon and procession. After he had stayed there five days, the boats set out again.

They had a difficult passage down the river. In some places, the river was very shallow, and their boats grounded on the bottom, whence they had to be released, with much poling and lifting, by the boatmen. In other places, the stream ran very swiftly through a tangle of over-leaning boughs, which they had to chop down. Luckily, a heavy rain swelled the river, and made their passage easier than it might have been.

The difficulty of navigating the Chagres was one of the strongest points in the defence system of Panama: the Spaniards relied upon it completely. This Gage and his companions discovered when, after twelve days, they reached the castle at its mouth. It was ready to fall to the ground. Apparently the Spaniards, thinking of the river as their ally, did not concern themselves with keeping the castle in good repair. The Governor of the castle, who was not only a drunkard, but a proselytizing one, plied them with wine all the time they were there. He tried to take Gage on as a chaplain, 'but greater matters called me further, and so I took my leave of him'. Regretfully, the governor let them go to their boats, after giving them 'some dainties of fresh meat, fish and conserves'.

On the morning of the next day, they reached Portobello.

Portobello was at once a very small and a very important town. Its permanent population was barely more than two thousand, yet it was, like Panama, one of the most important commercial centres of the Spanish Empire. Accordingly, it was fortified as if the king himself resided there.

First of all, it was the Caribbean terminus of the treasure route across the Isthmus of Panama. Here came the mule-trains from Panama, laden with bullion and jewels from Peru, which could be loaded at Portobello on to the ships of the Atlantic merchant fleet. Twice in the year, a great fair was held. It was in the form of an open-air bazaar; not only was unimaginable wealth in bullion and precious stones transhipped here, but goods poured in from all of Central America, and it was the great slave market of the area.

The town was protected by three castles, two of them at the mouth of the harbour, and another within. No ship, faced with such cross-fire, could force a passage. The town itself, which was almost two miles within the harbour, was almost an appendage of the citadel of Santiago de la Gloria, and was further protected by a smaller castle, San Jeronimo.

When Gage's small vessel penetrated the harbour, he was sorry to note that there were no great ships riding there. The longer the time before the galleons arrived from Spain, the more money he would have to spend, and he did not have much.

First he had to find lodgings. At that time, they were both plentiful and cheap; indeed, in more than one place he was offered lodgings for nothing, provided only he promised that, when the galleons came, he would either leave them or consent to pay very high rent for them. Over the forty days of the fair, shops might rent for, very roughly, the equivalent of £333 and large houses for £1666.

Luckily, Gage fell in with a 'kind gentleman', who, as it happened, was the King's Treasurer. This man promised that he would find him lodgings which would be cheap even after the fleet had come in. He accompanied Gage in his search, and made use of his authority when they spoke to landlords. They did, at last, find a tiny room: it was just big enough to hold a bed, a table, and a stool or two, 'with room enough besides to open and shut the door'. It rented, for the period of time the fleet was in Portobello, which was about a fortnight, for six-score crowns, about £40. It was, as we have seen, a small town; yet the fair brought a horde of wealthy merchants from Peru, Spain and other places, as well as the four or five thousand soldiers who guarded the fleet. Very often the town was not big enough to contain them all.

175

Gage himself knew of a merchant who, for fifteen days rental of a shop 'of reasonable bigness' in which to sell his wares, had paid a thousand crowns. But Gage was not a rich merchant, and he did not feel inclined to pay six-score crowns for a room which was nothing more than a mousehole. He threw himself on the mercy of the King's Treasurer, explaining that he had been lately robbed at sea, and could not afford to pay so much for rent alone, since it would leave him no money for food. The landlord, he added, would not cut his price by a farthing. The Treasurer, who does seem to have been an extraordinarily kind man, offered to pay half the rent, if Gage himself could pay the rest. Even this was difficult. Gage was released from his dilemma when another person—he does not say whom—offered him a room for nothing.

He then set out to make a little bit of money for himself, which he did by celebrating a few Masses, and preaching two sermons at fifty crowns apiece.

Gage dutifully visited the castles, but does not tell us anything other than that they were very strong. What did astonish him was the sight of mule-train after mule-train arriving from Panama, loaded down with wedges of silver. In one day, he counted two hundred mules laden with nothing but silver, and watched the wedges of precious metal being unloaded in the public market-place, where they lay 'like heaps of stones in the street, without any fear or suspicion of being lost'.

Within ten days the fleet came: eight galleons and ten merchant ships. Suddenly the streets, which had been quiet and drowsy, were filled with a gesticulating crowd.

Now prices began to climb, steeply and steadily. A fowl, which used to cost one real, now cost twelve; beef, which had cost half a real for thirteen pounds now cost two reals a pound. Even fish and tortoise-meat, the food of the poor, rose in price; and this was all he could afford. He marvelled to see how the merchants sold their commodities, not by the ell or yard, but by the piece or by weight, and to observe that they did not pay in coin, but in wedges of silver which were weighed and bartered like commodities. He was glad to see the wedges of silver disappearing into the bowels of the ships: the faster they were put aboard, the faster the ships would leave, and he with them. Not only was he running out of money; he had a justified fear of falling sick.

Portobello was a fever town at the best of times, and the arrival of so many people put a strain on its limited sanitary facilities. Gage describes it as 'an open grave'. In the year he was there, about five hundred of the merchants, soldiers and marines died of fevers, dysentery, and 'other disorders'. There was a large hospital in the town, with many friars 'whose calling and profession is only to cure and attend upon the sick, and to bear the dead unto their graves'.

The Admiral, Don Carlos de Ybarra (the same who had been in charge of the fleet when Gage had sailed from Cadiz twelve years earlier) was anxious to be gone. Since Gage was afraid of pirates, he thought it would be most prudent to book his passage in one of the biggest and strongest ships, but its captain would not accept him for less than three hundred crowns, which was more than he could afford. Once again, though, his friend the Treasurer came to his rescue. He commended him to the master of a merchant ship, the *San Sebastian*, who was, he knew, anxious to carry a chaplain with him at his own table. The master, in fact, consented to carry him for nothing, and to board him at his own table, only asking in return his prayers for a safe voyage. He offered further, some payment for any sermons Gage should preach in his ship. And Gage 'blessed God, acknowledging in this also His Providence, who in all occasions furthered my return to England'.

Thus Gage left America. The year was 1637. He had avoided, or escaped from, cannibals, sharks, the Inquisition, caymans, pirates and a fate worse than death in the Philippines. Later, he would return of his own free will to America, and he would die there.

XXI—*The Apostate*

A DAY or two before Christmas, in the year 1637, Gage finally landed at Dover. Two days later, he presented himself at the house of his kinswoman, Lady Penelope Gage. At first she did not recognize him. This is not strange. He had been away twenty-three years, having left England as a boy, and he was so unused to speaking English that he sounded, she told him, 'like an Indian or a Welshman'.

He had, with his usual bad luck, come home at an unfortunate time. The Great Rebellion was brewing.

All over Europe, new capitalists and old land-holding aristocrats were rising in revolt against the growing powers of centralized monarchy. In France, there would be the Fronde (1649–1653); in the Spanish Empire there would be the great Catalan revolt of 1640, the revolt of the Portuguese nobles in 1640, the attempt of the Duke of Medina-Sidonia and the Marquis of Ayamonte, in 1641, to make Andalusia an independent kingdom, and the Sicilian and Neopolitan revolts of 1647. Foreign powers took advantage of this chaos, and in the process created a complex web of international intrigue: Cromwell made overtures to Cardinal de Retz, one of the leaders of the Fronde: Richelieu helped to arouse the Covenanters against Charles the First, made an attempt to bring the Portuguese rebels under his wing, and put the armies of France on the side of the Catalan republicans; the Jesuits, in addition to preaching, if Voltaire is to be believed, the doctrine of justifiable regicide, supported the Portuguese actively and the Catalans passively; and the Jews financed all comers. The period coincided with a great revival of occultism, from complex hermetic philosophies to the crudities of witchcraft; and the age even had its own international 'philosophes', such as Hartlib, Dury and Comenius.

As in all revolutions, it was hard to tell the reactionaries from the radicals. Representatives of revolutionary capitalism justified themselves by an appeal to ancient privileges; advocates of that new thing in Europe, the monolithic state, fought in the name of loyalty to Church and Crown. Tradition and innovation fought on both sides, and sometimes in the same breast. In the intellectual wars which accompanied the political ones, there appeared the ancestors of almost all contemporary political and social doctrines.

In England, the situation was no less paradoxical and confusing than it was elsewhere. The Great Rebellion has been considered variously a lower-class revolt, a revolt of pragmatism against medieval obscurantism, a recrudescence of medieval millenarism, a capitalist rebellion, a baron's war, a Protestant uprising, and an English expression of an international revolutionary movement. Modern opinions on the matter are as contradictory as those on the French Revolution, and only the uninformed know exactly what happened. Even the actors in this bloody tragedy (or, if you will, glorious epic) stumbled through their parts without a clear idea of what the outcome would be. Cromwell's letters and speeches suggest a choking and sulphurous fog filled with muffled exclamations and the clash of weapons: to the Royalists, the rebellion was an overflowing of the social sewers. It is therefore not surprising that poor Gage, who had come home only to find the house on fire, should have suffered a kind of moral breakdown.

The first blow was the discovery that his father, who had died four years earlier, had indeed cut him out of his will. Gage, though a member of a rich and distinguished family, was penniless and despised in his own country. It is true that he would have protectors so long as he remained a friar. He was in contact with many of the English and Irish Dominicans, Benedictines and Jesuits who clustered around the wealthy English Romanists, and who frequented the court of Queen Henrietta Maria. Once he was arrested, but Sir Francis Windebanke, the Secretary of State, who sympathized with the Roman Catholics, intervened on his behalf. On the other hand, it seems he could not get along with his fellow Dominicans. The Provincial of the small Dominican community was one Thomas Middleton, or Dade. Gage, with two others, Popham and Craft, intrigued to have Middleton removed. Eventually a papal envoy came from Rome to settle the matter. His recommendation, a typically bureaucratic one, was that a new Provincial be appointed, and Gage removed to another area.

This information comes from the letters of George Conn, the Papal agent in England. Gage tells us nothing of the matter. He merely states that he sought and obtained permission to go to Rome, 'to confer some points' with the Master-General of his order. What these points were, we do not know; but one is inclined to be sceptical of Gage's claim that he wished to observe the Papist and Protestant churches of Europe, in order to resolve his doubts. It is more likely that he was still pursuing his 'career' in the Roman church.

He tells us, as it were by-the-by, that he was 'on some business' for his uncle, John Copley of Gatton.

Gage does not tell us what his uncle's business was, but it must have been an important matter. In 1639, we find him on his way to Rome. The governor of Dover Castle, on Gage's presenting him a letter from 'a Papist in London', allowed him to board the packet boat to Dunkirk without being searched. In Flanders, he met his brother Henry, who was stationed with the English Legion near Ghent, in the service of the Spanish crown. He also met his brother's chaplain, the Jesuit Father Peter Wright. This was to prove, for Wright, an unlucky encounter. Henry gave him a letter of recommendation to Don Rodrigo Pacheco Osorio, the Marqués de Serralvo, who was then at Brussels. The Marqués, and 'other great men', gave him letters to many important personages in Rome, among them Cardinals Cucua, Albornos and Barberini.

What was the business which was to bring the least distinguished member of the Gage family, a known runaway and trouble-maker, into the company of some of the greatest personages of Roman Catholic Europe? Francisco Barberini was an enormously powerful figure in Rome. He came from one of the great feudal families of Tuscany. He was the nephew of the Pope (Maffeo Barberini was Urban VIII), and his brothers were Taddeo Barberini, general of the papal forces, and Antonio Barberini, 'Protector of the Crown of France'. Francisco was himself styled 'Protector of the Crown of England'. As to the Marqués de Serralvo, he was that very viceroy who had landed with Gage at Vera Cruz; he had returned to Spain in 1635, much wealthier than he had been when he left. It is true, of course, that Gage's family connections could explain these encounters. It is quite possible that George Gage, who was well-known in Rome, was familiar with 'The Protector of England'; and Sir Henry and the Marqués de Serralvo were both in the service of the Spanish crown in the Low Countries. Yet one cannot help wishing that Gage had stated exactly what his uncle John's 'business' was.

There was much talk in Rome, Gage tells us, about Archbishop Laud. Laud, he would have us believe, was secretly a Roman Catholic. He must have known better. It is true that many Roman Catholics thought, at one time, that Laud might be won over: indeed, the Pope, as Laud himself recorded in his diary, had tempted him with the offer of a cardinal's hat. But it soon became clear to Rome that Laud was as Anglican as his king, and that the peace he desired with Rome was the peace of equals. Such confidence was more galling than the fury of the most rabid Calvinist; and Rome came to the conclusion that Laud meant, to use the words of a contemporary Roman Catholic Englishman, William Weston, 'to frame a motley religion of his own, and be lord of it himself'. Gage's statements about Laud are, in fact, Puritan propaganda, intended to justify his martyrdom as an act of justice.

He also passes along some gossip about a few noted recusants who were, he says, being considered for cardinalates. These were, he says, Sir William Hamilton, who was backed by 'a great number of friends', Sir Kenelm Digby, who was sponsored by Queen Henrietta Maria and assiduously puffed by his chaplain, Fitton, and two other prominent English papists—Walter Montague, son of the Earl of Manchester, and Sir Toby Matthew, a great friend of his brother George. Sir William Hamilton, however, had become involved with a woman, and was now out of the running.

This, while it may be factually true, is misleading. Gage, in his anxiety to condemn the English at Rome, does not tell us that Montague, Digby and Fitton were regarded with some suspicion by the Vatican. They were far from being orthodox. Digby was an occultist, and perhaps an early Freemason (in a paper read before the Royal Society in 1661, he would refer to God as the 'Supreme Architect'), and he used to hold seances with Walter Montague. Freemasonry, certainly, had not yet been condemned by Rome; but the trio also had well marked tendencies towards theological heresy, as Rome then defined it. In 1646, they would become open 'Blackloists', adherents to the programme of Thomas White, who wrote under the pseudonym of 'Blackloe', among others. White was a teacher of philosophy at Douai College, which, curiously enough, would later be headed by Thomas' half-brother Francis. White wanted a National English Catholic church free of Vatican control; he questioned the infallibility of the Pope, and declared that he should be obeyed only when he demanded nothing contrary to civil loyalties; he stated that Catholics should be at least passively obedient to all established secular power; he opposed the Inquisition; and he was strongly anti-Jesuit. 'Blackloism' was, for obvious reasons, unacceptable to Rome, and White's books were put on the Index. It was said by his enemies that White's 'English Jansenism' was simply a device to induce Cromwell to accept an English Catholic church based on such principles. Indeed, Digby later became Cromwell's confidant, and his go-between with Cardinal Mazarin.

One would be surprised if Gage was unaware of Rome's suspicions (he tells us that the candidates failed); but he was obviously confident that his readers would not know them. He did not lie to them; rather, he retailed truths in such a way as to imply falsehoods.

Gage surfaced, from this immersion in the deep and sombre pool of Roman intrigue, to return to England. He had already made up his mind, he says, to become an Anglican.

In 1642, he preached a sermon of recantation in St Paul's, in London. By 1648, when his book was published, he had 'resolved upon a choice for the Parliament cause'.

In 1642, Father Thomas Holland was brought to trial as a Roman Catholic priest who had said mass in England. It was Gage's testimony which convicted him: he had been a schoolmate of his at St Omer's. Father Holland was hanged, drawn and quartered at Tyburn, praying to the end for Gage's soul.

Frightened by the appearance of a Protestant fanatic in the midst of his family, Colonel Henry Gage promised his brother a thousand pounds if he would leave England, but Gage was not to be tempted, at this point, by money.

In 1643, Gage's testimony was responsible for the execution of Father Arthur Bell, a Franciscan.

During the next two years he worked on *The English-American, or A New Survey of the West Indies*, and in 1648 it was published.

The book was an immediate success. It contained an advertisement, in awkward and confused but at times oddly imaginative verse, by Thomas Chaloner, a Yorkshire businessman and adherent of 'the natural religion', who was powerful in the Commonwealth, and was to become infamous as one of the regicides. Furthermore, Gage was now. rector of Acrise, a small parish in Kent, and he had taken a wife 'to satisfy the world of my sincerity'. Things were going well for him.

In his dedication to Lord Fairfax, 'Captain-General of the Parliament's Army', Gage sets out the reasons why he thinks his book might be 'to the use and benefit of my English countrymen'. Its main purpose, we discover, is to serve as a guidebook for an invading army.

He then discusses the reasons which might justify an English invasion of Spanish America.

These are well-considered and concisely expressed, though completely unoriginal. Such an enterprise would occupy the men of Cromwell's army after 'The settlement of the peace of this kingdom, and reduction of Ireland', and would ensure that their idleness 'may neither be a burden to themselves not the kingdom'. Englishmen, having established plantations in Barbados and other Caribbean islands, had become adapted to the climate, and were, in any case, more than halfway there. The conquest would be easy; witness the success of the Dutch against the Spaniards.

He then examines the objection, 'that the Spaniard being entitled to those countries, it were both unlawful and against all conscience, to dispossess him thereof'. Against this, he sets an argument with which we are all familiar: he disguises imperialism as anti-imperialism. 'No question but the just right or title to those countries appertains to the natives themselves, who, if they shall willingly and freely invite the English to their protection, what title soever they have in them no doubt they may legally transfer it or communicate it to others.' The Spaniards have no rights of ownership, but those based, first, on 'discovery', which in no way justifies the seizure of the 'discovered' lands from those who truly own it, and second, on force, which must yield to greater force. Furthermore, the atrocities committed by the Spaniards have invalidated their claim that they have a right to the possession of the New World, because of the moral superiority of their civilization over that of the Aztecs and other Indian peoples. Finally, as to the land unoccupied by either Spaniards or Indians, England has as much right to it as does any other power.

We may recognize here, briefly expressed, some of the

leading ideas of the imperialist party, ideas which had altered little from Elizabethan times. The hoped-for conquest of Spanish America, either by military or by economic means, was to be an important factor in British foreign policy to the days of Pitt. At the end of the sixteenth and beginning of the seventeenth centuries, its chief intellectual spokesmen were Raleigh, the Hakluyts and Bacon, who were supported by a horde of pamphleteers. Most of its practical support came from merchants interested in trans-Atlantic trade, a group particularly concentrated in the Virginia and Providence Island Companies. It was in these circles, also, that revolutionary feeling was concentrated. Christopher Hill, the historian, has described the Providence Island Company as 'a cover-organization for the Parliamentary opposition to Charles'. Three other groups were also interested in the conquest of Spanish America—the New England merchants, who had connections with the above-mentioned group, the planters of Barbados, and the Marranos, who had substantial interests in Barbados, the maritime trade of New England, and Spanish America. Cromwell himself had been a close associate of the founders of the Providence Island Company, and had been a member of the parliamentary commission for Plantations.

Before Gage was to receive the patronage of such exalted circles, however, he was to commit one act which has made his name infamous.

In 1651, there took place the trials of Fathers Middleton and Peter Wright. The last-named was Sir Henry's chaplain, and the man who had comforted him as he lay dying for his king near Oxford: Sir Henry had come over to England to fight for Charles. Gage was commanded to come up to London to give evidence.

He argued that while Father Middleton was a friar, he

was not a priest, and as a result of this testimony Father Middleton was acquitted. When he testified against Father Wright, though, he behaved in an altogether different manner, at least according to the report which has come down to us. One witness describes him as raving for nearly thirty minutes 'in so violent and marked a manner that it was evident from the beginning that he was instigated by hatred and a thirst for blood'. His own brother, he said, had planned his murder, and Father Wright, though he had heard of the plan in the confessional, had done nothing to prevent it. Father Wright declared he knew nothing of such a plan; nevertheless, he was executed at Tyburn on the tenth of May, 1651.

George Gage had already done his best to dissuade his brother from giving such damaging testimony. George had gone, says a Jesuit historian, 'to the haunt of vice where the wretched debauchee was lodging . . . to warn him of the divine judgments that were hanging over him if he should make himself guilty of innocent blood'. This 'haunt of vice' was, presumably, Gage's home.

In 1652, the Reverend George Gage was himself put in prison, where he later died. In a bill against him for appearance before the courts, Thomas is cited as an informer against him. There is no evidence that Thomas was heard in court, and Gage's editor, Thompson, has suggested that the bill might have been referring to information gleaned from his book. However, it must be admitted as unlikely that, if information was gleaned in this roundabout manner, a court document would not make some reference to the fact.

Gage's behaviour at this stage in his life is most puzzling. So far we have seen him to be hypocritical in his religion, and venal and unscrupulous in money matters; on the other hand he has shown that he could be generous to those

187

dependent on him, and that he was not uncourageous. We have even seen him to be, if only occasionally, a man of conscience.

There is no doubt that Gage felt he was testifying against the instruments of a criminal conspiracy. There is no doubt also that his new Puritan friends considered him, not a traitor, but 'a brand snatched from the burning'. Certainly the aims of the Roman Catholic activists of the time were all too clearly treasonable, and were recognized as such by most Englishmen, whether they were Puritans or not. Gage felt that his testimony put him in danger of death; and, indeed, he asked the court to protect him against attempts on his life, a request which was not granted. As to his 'thirst for blood', most of the accounts of his behaviour at the trials come from Jesuit and Dominican historians, from whom objectivity can hardly be expected. Gage cannot, after all, have been actuated entirely by malice, since he saved the life of Father Middleton, with whom he had quarrelled. He may also be forgiven if his sense of family solidarity had been somewhat weakened. Not only had his father cut him off without a penny, but his brother had tried to have him killed.

'What I have been able to discover for the good of this state I have done, and not spared (when called upon) to give in true evidence upon my oath against Jesuits, priests and friars; for the which (after a fair invitation from my brother Colonel Gage to come over again to Flanders, offering me a thousand pound ready money) I have been once assaulted in Aldersgate Street; and another time like to be killed in Shoe Lane by a captain of my brother's regiment, named Vincent Burton, who (as I was after informed) came from Flanders on purpose to make me away or convey me over, and with such a malicious design followed me to my lodging, lifting up the latch and opening the door (as he had seen me do) and attempting to go up the stairs to my chamber without any enquiry for me, or knocking at the door; from which God graciously delivered me by the weak means of a woman my landlady, who stopped him from going any further; and being demanded his name, and answering by the name of Stewart, and my landlady telling him from me that I knew him not, he went away chafing and saying that I should know him before he had done with me. But he that knoweth God well shall know no enemy to his hurt; neither have I never since seen or known this man. I might here also write down the contents of a threatening letter from mine own brother, when he was colonel for the King of England and governor of Oxford, but forbear to do so out of some tender considerations of flesh and blood . . .'

This said, however, his actions at this time remain inexplicable. The most favourable adjective one could apply to them, even considering all the pressures to which he was subject, would be 'contemptible'; and perhaps a much stronger adjective would be more appropriate.

In 1654, Cromwell, having reduced the Irish and almost everything and everyone else ('The Lord is pleased still to vouchsafe us His presence, and to prosper His own work in our hands'), began to dream of Empire. As he was to say two years later, in one of those curiously murky speeches of his:

'The Spaniard is your enemy; and your enemy, as I tell you, naturally, by that antipathy which is in him— providentially, and this in divers respects. You could not get an honest or honourable peace from him; it was sought by the Long Parliament; it was not attained. It could not be attained with honour and honesty. I say, it could not be attained with honour and honesty. And truly, when I say that, he is naturally throughout an enemy; an enmity is put into him by God. "I will put an enmity between thy seed and her seed"; which goes but for little among statesmen, but is more considerable than all things! And he that considers not such natural enmity the providential enmity, as well as the accidental, I think he is not well acquainted with Scripture and the things of God. And the Spaniard is not only our enemy accidentally, but he is providentially so, God having in His wisdom disposed it so to be, when we made a breach with the Spanish nation.'

Gage, perhaps on Chaloner's recommendation, was asked to prepare a memorandum on the prospects of success of an invasion of Spanish America. He did so; and the gist of it was that conquest would be very easy. All the arguments were in his book. We have seen the main reasons for Cromwell's interest in this scheme; but a further reason is given by Bishop Burnet, in his *History of His Own Times*: 'By this he reckoned he would be supplied with such a treasure, that his government would be established before he should need to have any recourse to a parliament for money.'

The Venetian ambassador in London informed his government that plans were being laid for an attack, based on 'the information of a Dominican friar who has been in those parts, and knows them well, who has had many secret conferences with the Protector on the subject'. And one Stoupe, coming in upon Cromwell one day, saw him examining, with loving attention, a chart of the Gulf of Mexico.

Milton, who was of course a civil servant at the time, was to write a tract, in which he contended:

'that the motives whereby we have been lately induced to make an attack upon certain islands in the West Indies which have been now for some time in the hands of the Spaniards are exceeding just and reasonable, every one will easily see who considers in what a hostile manner that king and his subjects have all alone, in those parts of America, treated the English nation . . .'

In December of 1654, the invasion fleet left Portsmouth, under sealed orders. A declaration of war would not follow until December 1655; Cromwell did not believe in giving his enemies the advantage of a warning. (The advantage of fighting with the forces of Anti-Christ, as compared to those of fighting with only relatively evil men, is that one is not compelled to observe the niceties of war.) There were sixty ships, and four thousand soldiers, which last number was augmented, at Barbados, to a number estimated by various historians as being from 6,680 to 9,000.

Gage was chaplain to General Robert Venables, who was, with Admiral William Penn, co-commander of the expedition. Their objective was Hispaniola.

The attempt to invade Hispaniola was, however, a disaster.

To begin with, the soldiers were on the verge of mutiny. They were not to be allowed any booty: gold and plate was to be turned over to their officers, to be put away for the Lord Protector. Their reward was to be miserly in the extreme: six weeks extra pay.

The officers, by a combination of threats and promises, finally got the troops ashore. They came across an Irishman, and asked him to lead them to a spring, where they might fill their water-casks. But he led them straight to a Spanish fort, and when the Spaniards opened fire, General Venables hid behind a tree.

Later encounters were equally disastrous.

No doubt Venables blamed Gage for the complete failure of the invasion. Gage had argued that the negroes of Hispaniola would immediately ally themselves with the English against their Spanish masters. In fact, however, the negroes had proved loyal: their masters had promised them their freedom if they fought, and had persuaded them, moreover, that the English were cannibals. As for the Spaniards, they fought with supreme confidence, since they had indulgences hanging about their necks, pardoning them from all sins past and to come.

The British had withdrawn and camped on the beach. There were many wild cattle roaming in the forest, but they were afraid to enter it. After a while, since they were on the verge of starvation, they began to eat their own dogs and horses. At night the land crabs came down to the sea to feed, and the British, hearing the clicking of their legs and thinking them the rattling of bandoliers, ran into the sea. They shot at fire-flies, thinking them the lights of the enemy.

When they began to come down with various tropical diseases, they put it to General Venables that they should leave Hispaniola and try Jamaica instead. They left behind them a few Spanish dead, and a desecrated image of the Virgin Mary, which they had pelted with oranges.

The behaviour of this pathetic rabble need not surprise us. Consider who composed it. The two thousand five hundred Englishmen were mostly the dregs of the Parliamentary army, or vagabonds who had been recruited by force and given no military training whatsoever. With them were an undetermined number of beachcombers, failed planters, and unsatisfactory servants from Barbados and other West Indian islands.

Not all of them were of British stock, however. The pilot, Campoe Sabbatha (or Sibada) was a Marrano from Antigua, and another Marrano, Acosta, was in charge of the commissariat.

There were also some proto-Americans. For example, Robert Sedgwick, the merchant from Charleston, was a Major-General in the expedition.

Had Gage stood upon the deck of the flagship as the fleet entered what is now Kingston Harbour, he would have seen no sign of a city. Where the port is now, he would have seen only bush, and the mangroves growing into the shallow water, a wave-lapped thicket of roots. The only sign of human occupation was Passage Fort, an unimpressive fortification.

The *Martin*, with twelve guns and a crew of sixty, was one of the smallest ships in the fleet. But, of the few shots it fired into the fort, one disabled a Spanish major, the best soldier there. The *Martin* was run ashore, and its men disembarked. The Spanish defenders fled, leaving three guns mounted in the fort. In the taking of Passage Fort, not one English life was lost.

When the soldiers had landed, they marched through a wood until they came to the edge of the savannah. Their prize, Santiago de la Vega, was only a quarter of a mile away. It was an attractive town of some nine hundred houses. The houses were simple enough. They were rambling single-storey structures, made of the split trunks of cabbage palms, or of reed overcast with mortar and lime, and roofed with tiles or palmetto thatch. There were six notable structures —five churches and a Franciscan cloister. Santiago de la Vega was laid out in the grid-pattern typical of Spanish colonial towns, and the houses were, except for those around the market-place, set far apart. It was deserted: the Spaniards had buried their treasures, turned their livestock loose, and fled to the north.

The British sacked and burned the town, and melted down the church bells to make bullets.

What were Gage's feelings when he saw the destruction of Santiago de la Vega? Did he have qualms of conscience? Did he think pleasantly of the land grant which would come to him as one of the pioneers in the conquest of Jamaica? Was he proud or ashamed of his role in the action; and did he still feel, as he had said in his book, that God had made use of him 'as a Joseph to discover the treasures of Egypt'? How had he felt when, in Hispaniola, the soldiers had splattered with oranges the statue of the Virgin Mary, with the infant Lord in her arms? Had he remembered, perhaps, a more innocent game in a little town near Chiapa de Corzo, when he and his friends had thrown oranges at the sub-deacon Juan Escudero?

We do not know. All we know is that Thomas Gage died in Jamaica early in 1656. The island was still ruled by military law, and there were no other clergymen, since the other chaplain, William Dennys, had died already. Gage's death was, in all probability, not an easy one.

In November, 1655, a few months before Gage died, a member of the expedition, whose name has now been lost, wrote the following letter home—

'The eleven ships lately arrived at this place with &c. poor men I pity them at the heart, all their imaginary mountains of gold are turned into dross, and their reason and affections are ready to bid them sail home again already. For my part, greater disappointments I never met with, having had no provision allowed me in ten weeks last past, or above three biscuits this fourteen weeks, so that all I can rake and scrape in ready money goes to housekeeping, and the shifts I make are not to be written here. We have lost half our army from our first landing in Spaniola, when we were eight thousand, besides one thousand or more seamen in arms. Never did my eyes see such a sickly time, nor so many funeral and graves all the town over that it is a very Golgotha. We have a savannah or plain near us where some of the soldiers are buried so shallow that the Spanish dogs, which lurk about the town, scrape them up and eat them. As for English dogs, they are most eaten by our soldiery; not one walks the streets that is not shot at, unless well befriended and respected. We have not only eaten all the cattle within twelve miles of the place, but now almost all the horses, asses, mules' flesh near us, so that I shall hold little Eastcheap in more esteem than the whole Indies if this trade last, and I can give nor learn no reason that it should not here continue; so beside this we expect no pay here, nor hardly at home now, but perhaps some ragged land at the best, and that but by the by spoken of, for us general officers not a word mentioned. I could dwell long upon this subject, and could tell you that still half our army lies sick and helpless, nor had we victuals for them before this fleet, nor expect aught now save some bread, and bran, and oatmeal, and if that with physic will not keep them alive, we have no other remedy but death for them. For my own part in twenty-five years have I not endured so much sickness as here with bloody flux, rheum, ague, fever, so that I desire earnestly to go for England in March next, if permitted, for I am fallen away five inches about.'

It was in surroundings such as this that Gage died. We do not know the cause of his death, but it might have been one of the diseases which were then sweeping through the army of invasion. He did not even have the satisfaction of knowing that, when the news of Jamaica's fall reached Mexico, all the church bells of the viceregal capital tolled in mourning.

It was, if belated and unsatisfactory, some kind of recognition.

Appendix

Was Gage a Spy?

CERTAIN inconsistencies in Gage's story suggest ambiguities in his motives in going to Mexico. I may be unduly suspicious in noting these, but at least they occasion interesting speculations.

It must be admitted, at the beginning, that it is unlikely that the questions I raise here will ever be solved. The fact is that the little evidence we have concerning Gage's early life is contradictory. We do not know the exact year of his birth; and indeed we cannot even be sure of his place of birth: some sources say he was born in Ireland. In his deposition against Thomas Holland, Gage stated that he and Holland had studied together for five years at St Omer's, a statement Holland did not deny. This would mean that Gage was at St Omer's between 1615 and 1621, as Holland is known to have been. However, there is other evidence which seems to indicate that Gage was studying theology in Spain in 1615. (In his book, *A Hundred Homeless Years*, Father Godfrey Anstruther, O.P., goes into the chronology of Gage's early life at some length.)

We need not read, into this confusion of dates, a deliberate attempt at obfuscation. It simply indicates the unreliability of much apparently 'hard' documentary evidence. To illustrate this point, let us take the evidence relating to the arrival in Mexico of the Marqués de Serralvo, who, Gage says, landed with him in Vera Cruz on the twelfth of September,

1625. One respectable Mexican historian says Serralvo arrived on the third of November, 1624; one of the best United States authorities on colonial Mexican history has him arriving in November of 1626; another U.S. authority in this field seems to believe he was well established in Mexico in 1624. When there is so much confusion concerning an important event in Mexican history, we have no right to expect complete certainty in the biography of an obscure Dominican friar.

We cannot be sure, therefore, of the dates we have. Least of all can we be sure of Gage's exact age. This should be kept in mind when considering the speculation that follows.

Thompson, in his introduction to his edition of the *Travels*, points out that the records of the Privy Council for 1616–17 state that a certain Thomas Gage had been arrested in 1617, held incommunicado as 'a dangerous man', and brought before the Privy Council. A. P. Newton believes this was our Thomas Gage, that he had come back to England to see his family, and that he was arrested because it was known he was returning to St Omer. 'After a few days detention', Newton says, 'he was released, and went back to his studies.' Thompson believes this could not have been Gage, who was, he says, only fourteen or fifteen at the time, and thus hardly a 'man': in any case, he adds, students at St Omer did not return to England until their studies were completed. He thinks that somebody else may have assumed the name 'Gage', since it was common for travelling recusants and priests to adopt non-existent names, or to exchange names, to confuse the authorities.

This is certainly logical. However, the assumption that Gage was only in his mid-teens at the time is based on deductions and probabilities, rather than a sure knowledge of the facts: it is equally possible that he was in his late teens in 1617, since his exact birth-date is not known. Furthermore, if Gage was only in his mid-teens in 1617, then he would have been too young in 1625 to have become a Jesuit. Thus his father's action in 1625—cutting him out of his will for antagonism to the Jesuits—would have seemed excessive, as Thompson himself says. Thompson suggests that Thomas had given out 'recriminations and perhaps sensational charges against the order which would be given added emphasis by enemies of the Papacy because they had been uttered by a member of one of the prominent families of England that had stood by the old faith and suffered for it'. But the action would still have been excessive, if Gage had simply slandered the order in conversation, particularly if he was not a member of the order, and was still a boy.

Furthermore, Gage's fears that he would be completely scorned by his friends and kindred if he returned to England would seem a baseless hysteria, if he had only refused to become a Jesuit, even if this was accompanied by boyish complaints against the order. The rivalry between religious orders in the seventeenth century is well known: one did not cease to become a good Roman Catholic by hating the Jesuits.

One cannot help suspecting that Gage had, in some manner, done serious harm to the Roman Catholic cause.

Christopher Devlin's life of Robert Southwell, though it deals with the reign of Elizabeth, an earlier time, is enlightening on the methods used by English agents to frustrate the work of the Jesuits.

For one thing, they always approached monks and friars who had differences with their superiors: Gage had a notably rebellious and factious spirit, as research into his life clearly shows.

Devlin believes that the playwright, Gosson, was rewarded for his spying by being made rector in the Parish Church at

Stepney. Gage, after he left the Roman Church, was given the church of Acrise, in Kent.

Could the 'dangerous man' taken in 1617 really have been our Thomas Gage, and could he then have been encouraged to act as a counter-intelligence agent for Protestant England? Could his father have heard of this in some way? If this were true (and I must emphasize that this is only a wild hypothesis), it would account for his black rage against his son, which would seem excessive in view of the facts as Gage presents them. Certainly, it was not uncommon for the government to capture suspected priests, and release them on assurance that they would provide them with information.

My suspicion was first aroused by Gage's extraordinarily vivid and careful descriptions. The book was published in 1648, eleven years after he left America. I find it difficult to believe that, unless he had a photographic memory, he could have remembered what he did. He must have taken notes as he went, since there were few books of Mexican geography to which he could return to refresh his memory. Why did he take notes?

Note-takers are not necessarily spies, one might say, and this is perfectly true. To this one might respond, though, that he seems to have made the kind of notes one would expect a spy to make. He makes a careful analysis of the economic state of the country: he notes major roads and navigable rivers, gives an estimate of the population of various cities, towns and villages, and is precise on the details of fortifications. If all travelling friars had had his strategic sense, the entire world would have been Roman Catholic long ago.

The closing paragraph of his book is significant—

'I shall think my time and pen happily employed if by

what here I have written I may strengthen the perusers of this small volume against Popish superstition whether in England, other parts of Europe, Asia or America; for the which I shall offer up my daily prayers unto Him, Who (as I may well say) miraculously brought me from America to England, and hath made use of me as a Joseph to discover the treasures of Egypt, or as the spies to search into the land of Canaan, even the God of all nations, to Whom be ascribed by me and all true and faithful believers, Glory, Power, Majesty and Mercy for evermore. Amen.'

Having said all this, I must say that my own opinion is that he was certainly not a spy in the sense that he was secretly in the pay of his government from the beginning. Admittedly, the matter could not be decided until we know what went on in that Privy Council meeting in 1617. But his long stay in the unimportant villages of Mixco and Pinola does not suggest that he was gathering intelligence on his government's orders.

I am inclined to think that he was, as a spy, self-employed. I feel that he became disillusioned with Roman Catholicism quite early, that his stay in America completed the process, and that he was not unaware of the possibility that, if the worst came to the worst, his notes could be put to use if he left the Church. I would say that in Guatemala he actively began thinking that his notes might be of use to the British Government, since it is at this point that he begins noticing fortifications and possible invasion routes, not with the idle speculations of a traveller, but in a more conscious and detailed way. It is in Guatemala that 'four-eyed Hidalgo' (he may not merely be referring to his glasses) suggests that he might be a spy and a heretic, and it is here that he makes the acquaintance of Antonio Fernandez, the 'Portuguese' merchant, who departs from Guatemala 'for some reasons which here I must conceal'. Here also he begins to show some knowledge of Lutheran and Calvinist doctrine, though it must be said that he could have acquired some knowledge of these doctrines by reading Papist arguments against them. In his book *The Fall of the Spanish-American Empire*, Salvador de Madariaga has said (with adequate supporting documentation), 'The Jews were assiduous agents in the dissemination of the Reformation, less out of any genuine interest in the Reformation as such than because it implied a schism and a division in the rival faith' (p. 248).

Furthermore, as is well known, the Marranos in both America and Europe, hating the Roman Catholicism of the Inquisition, did all they could to advance a possible invasion of the Spanish New World by Cromwellian England. Cromwell's Jewish intelligencers—the merchants Carvajal, de Caceres and Dormido—gave him access to extensive and speedy information about the affairs of the New World. Before Cromwell came on the scene, the 'Portuguese' of the New World, and the great Marrano mercantile houses of Europe had been conspiring with the Dutch to the same end.

In other words, Gage's 'Portuguese' friends in Guatemala may have helped him to become a Protestant, and may themselves have engaged in undercover activities.

Rydjord (see Bibliography) has pointed out the role played by the Portuguese in the fomenting of sedition in New Spain, particularly in the 1640's, when Portugal was fighting for her independence. The Inquisition, indeed, imprisoned many Portuguese at this time, so many that the prisons could not hold them all.

The viceroy at this time was Don Diego Lopéz Pacheco Cabrera y Bobadilla, Duque de Escalona and Marqués de Villena; and there were stories that he had talked of making himself king of New Spain. He was, it was well known, a cousin of the Duke of Braganza, who had seized the throne of Portugal. He had distributed pamphlets, pointing out the relationship of the House of Pacheco to the royal families of England, Savoy, Modena and Spain itself. His enemies grumbled at his garrisoning the country's most strategic port, San Juan de Ulloa, with Portuguese soldiers; and, by a curious coincidence, a shipment of treasure from the viceroy arrived in Portugal just as that country rose in revolt. Finally, his bishop, Palafox, suspected him of wanting to set up an independent dynasty in New Spain. In 1643, the Duke of Escalona was removed from his post without warning, and sent to Spain to explain his actions. Philip the Fourth, fully satisfied with his explanation, named him the new viceroy of Sicily, which revolted in 1647.

One would love to know the full title of the 'Duke of Medina', who was aware of the fact that this obscure English friar was sailing to America, and tried, if ineffectually, to prevent his departure. Unfortunately, there were three dukes of this title prominent in the public life of the time—Medina de Rioseco, Medina-Sidonia and Medina de las Torres—and we do not know which 'Medina' Gage is referring to, though the most likely candidate is Medina-Sidonia. Medina-Sidonia, brother of the Queen of Portugal, later hoped—with the help of the Portuguese rebels—to make himself king of an independent Andalusia. Curiously enough, though the island of Jamaica was held in fief by the Dukes of Veragua (the descendants of Columbus, a title which died out, in the direct male line, with Diego Columbus), Henry Whistler, in his *Journal of the West Indian Expedition 1654–55*, says Jamaica belongs to 'the Duke of Meden' (Williams—p. 287).

However, this is all speculation: the facts here gathered can be explained, individually at least. Only an expert in the diplomatic history of the Cromwellian period could properly evaluate them. Even if it hangs together as an argument, and helps to explain certain inconsistencies in Gage's narrative, it by no means follows that the tidiest explanation is the true one. Life and art are two quite separate things; real people are seldom consistent, and attempts to explain loose ends in their behaviour can often lead, I readily admit, to a picture which may pervert the untidy reality into a neat work of the rational imagination.

Acknowledgements and Select Bibliography

I am indebted to Father Godfrey Anstruther, O.P., author of *A Hundred Homeless Years*, for some of the quotations from Dominican documents concerning Gage.

EDITIONS OF GAGE'S TRAVELS

I am greatly indebted to two excellent editions of Gage's travels. One of these, *Thomas Gage's Travels in the New World*, was prepared by the noted archaeologist, J. Eric S. Thompson, and published by the University of Oklahoma Press in 1958. This edition is full of new and interesting material on Gage, much more than I have been able to incorporate in this brief book. The other, *Thomas Gage: The English-American*, was prepared by A. P. Newton, and published by Routledge in London in 1928, in the *Broadway Travellers* series. It is from this that my quotations from Gage himself are taken, with the kind permission of the publishers. Though Thompson's research has invalidated one or two of Newton's points, his edition is still valuable, since it presents some material for which Thompson had no room, and is enlivened by an excellent introduction and some charming prints. Newton's edition is, on the whole, more faithful to Gage's text: Thompson has, for the sake of readability, cut up Gage's exasperatingly long sentences, and rationalized his often confusing grammar.

GENERAL

AKRIGG, G. P. V.: *Jacobean Pageant, The Court of King James I*: Harvard University Press, Cambridge, Mass., 1962

ALAMÁN, Lucas: *Obras*: Editorial Jus, Mexico D.F., 1942

ANONYMOUS: *Annals of the Cakchiquels* (trans. Recinos and Goetz): University of Oklahoma Press, Norman, Oklahoma, 1953

ANONYMOUS: *Popol Vuh* (trans. Recinos, Goetz and Morley): William Hodge and Co. Ltd, London, 1951

ANSTRUTHER, Father Godfrey, O. P.: *A Hundred Homeless Years*: Blackfriar's Press, London, 1959

BALBUENA, Bernardo de: *Grandeza de Mexico (La Grandeza Mexicana)*: Imprenta Universitaria, Mexico D.F.

ACKNOWLEDGEMENTS AND SELECT BIBLIOGRAPHY

BARBOUR, Violet: *Capitalism in Amsterdam in the Seventeenth Century*: University of Michigan Press, 1963

BOURNE, Edward Gaylord: *Spain in America, 1450–1580*: Barnes and Noble Inc., New York, 1962

BURNS, Sir Alan: *History of the British West Indies*: George Allen and Unwin Ltd, London, 1954

CROMWELL, Oliver: *Letters and Speeches* (ed. Carlyle): Routledge and Sons, London, 1888

CUNDALL, Frank: *Historic Jamaica*: Published for the Institute of Jamaica by the West India Committee: London, 1915

DAVIES, R. Trevor: *Spain in Decline, 1621–1700*: Macmillan and Co. Ltd, London, 1957

DEVLIN, Christopher: *The Life of Robert Southwell*: Longmans, London, 1956

DIAZ DEL CASTILLO, Bernal: *Historia Verdadera de la Conquista de la Nueva Espana*: Espasa-Calpe Argentina S.A., Mexico D.F., 1965

GALINDO Y VILLA: Jesus: *Historia Sumaria de la Ciudad de Mexico*: Editora Nacional S.A., Mexico D.F., 1955

GERARD, John: *John Gerard, The Autobiography of an Elizabethan*: (trans. Philip Caraman): Longmans, London, 1951

HARING, C. H.: *The Spanish Empire in America*: Harcourt Brace and World Inc., New York, 1952

HILL, Christopher: *The Century of Revolution*: Nelson and Sons Ltd, Edinburgh, 1962

HILL, Christopher: *Intellectual Origins of the English Revolution*: Oxford University Press, 1965

Historia Documental de Mexico: Universidad Nacional Autonoma de Mexico, Mexico, D.F., 1964

JESSE, John Heneage Jesse: *London, Her Crowned and Uncrowned, from Westminster to the Tower*: Nicholls and Co, London, undated

LEONARD, Irving A.: *Baroque Times in old Mexico*: University of Michigan Press, 1959

MADARIAGA, Salvador de: *The Fall of the Spanish-American Empire:* Hollis and Carter, London, 1947

MAYER, William: *Early Travellers in Mexico*: Mexico D.F., 1961 (privately printed)

PETERSON, R. T.: *Sir Kenelm Digby*: Jonathan Cape, London, 1956

RICARD, Robert: *The Spiritual Conquest of Mexico* (trans. Simpson): University of California Press, Berkeley, California, 1966

ROTH, Cecil: *A History of the Marranos*: Harper and Row, New York, 1966

RYDJORD, John: *Foreign Interest in the Independence of New Spain*: Duke University Press, Durham, North Carolina, 1935

SCHOLES, France V. and ROYS, Ralph L.: *Fray Diego de Landa and The Problem of Idolatry in Yucatan*: Carnegie Institute of Washington, 1938

SCHURZ, William Lytle: *The Manilla Galleon*: Dutton, New York, 1939

SIMPSON, Lesley Byrd: *Many Mexicos*: University of California Press, 1966

TREVELYAN, G. M.: *England Under the Stuarts*: Penguin Books, Harmondsworth, Middlesex, 1960

WILLIAMS, Eric (Ed.): *Documents of West Indian History 1492–1655*: PNM Publishing Co. Ltd, Port-of-Spain, Trinidad, 1963

ZAMACOIS, Niceto de: *Historia de Mexico* (Vol. 5): J. F. Parres y Cla: Mexico D.F., 1878

Index

209